"The Fresh Expressions movement is one of God's most hopeful pathways in the renewal of the church. Both Jorge Acevedo and Michael Beck have been at the heart of this story. And Michael Beck is emerging as an essential interpreter for us all. This field guide is faithful to our tradition, and it provokes us toward the world that God loves and seeks to redeem."

—Ken Carter, resident bishop, Florida Conference, president, Council of Bishops, The United Methodist Church

"Michael Beck is a force of nature. He is catalyzing at pace innovative Christian communities among people who do not currently attend church. He is a voice of the future. You can't afford to miss what he says!"

—Michael Moynagh, Wycliffe Hall, Oxford, UK, consultant on theology and practice to Fresh Expressions

"John Wesley took the gospel down (in prestige) and out (to the fringes of society), which is where innovation begins. You know something is innovative by three measures: (a) if it is fully functioning, (b) if it works for a long time, and (c) if it is the basis for subsequent innovation. Wesley's method checked all the boxes, and now so does Beck's field guide. In these pages you will find actual, real-world, functioning methods to make the gospel fresh to today people in today places."

—Len Wilson, creative and communications director, St. Andrew United Methodist Church, Plano, TX; author, *Think Like a Five Year Old*

"Rooted deeply in the Wesleyan tradition, a biblical and theological foundation for the Fresh Expressions movement challenges us to become more vile in order to become more vital. Personal accounts offer dramatic illustrations of the way the Spirit of God is wildly at work in the lives of real people in real places. It's a witness of hope for the future of the church."

—Jim Harnish, author, *A Disciple's Path*

"John Wesley would be happy to see a field guide for the renewal of Methodism since so much of his ministry was in the field. This book invites us to be instruments of renewal in our day just as the first Methodists were in theirs, and it provides excellent guidance in what such renewal might look like."

—Steve Harper, author, *Five Marks of a Methodist*

Michael Adam Beck
with Jorge Acevedo

A FIELD GUIDE TO

METHODIST

FRESH EXPRESSIONS

Abingdon Press
Nashville

A FIELD GUIDE TO METHODIST FRESH EXPRESSIONS
Copyright © 2020 by Abingdon Press

ISBN: 978-1-5018-9909-6
Library of Congress Control Number: 2020933055

20 21 22 23 24 25 26 27 28 29—10 9 8 7 6 5 4 3 2 1
MANUFACTURED IN THE UNITED STATES OF AMERICA

Menu

Foreword

Years ago, I was listening to a well-known Southern Baptist author and speaker. He was just beginning his talk when he used the phrase, "as I go about persecuting the church." His words elicited cautious laughter from the crowd. This gifted communicator was, tongue-in-cheek, comparing himself to Saul of Tarsus, persecutor of the church.[1] And having read and listened to this man, his self-description was accurate. He was being used by the Holy Spirit to "inflict" much-needed pain to awaken the slumbering church of Jesus in North America.

My friend, Michael Beck, is a "persecutor of the church" too. You see, Michael is an APE. In one of Paul's lists of spiritual gifts, he lists five gift offices: "the apostles, the prophets, the evangelists, the shepherds and teachers" (Eph 4:11 ESV). The acronym APE stands for the first three: apostle, prophet, evangelist. The propensity of the church that most often is led by the last two on Paul's list, shepherds and teachers, is to try and either domesticate the APEs or get rid of them. Michael has resisted both options.

Instead, with a love for the established and inherited church (so much so that he still co-pastors a local church with his wife), Michael has become a champion for and a "thorn in the flesh" to the church to awaken it to a fresh and new wave and work of the Holy Spirit. He still profoundly believes in the local church.

---

1. See Acts 8:1-3.

I, on the other hand, am a shepherd and teacher to the core. I resonate more with founder John Wesley and his struggle with field preaching as a method to reach pre-Christian people of the 1700s. Twenty years after beginning field preaching as a method to reach people, Wesley wrote:

> What marvel the devil does not love field preaching? Neither do I. I love a commodious room, a soft cushion, a handsome pulpit. But where is my zeal if I do not trample all these under foot in order to save one more soul?[2]

Left to my own devices, I am much more comfortable with the twenty-first-century version of the "commodious room": cool preaching podiums, flashing lights, drum cages, and comfy seats. Yet here's my humble confession. After twenty-three years in the same church, our teams discovered that an attractional church, which had brilliantly worked for us during the first fifteen years, dramatically slowed down since the Great Recession in its effectiveness to reach pre-Christian people for Jesus.

When it comes to fresh expressions of church as a missional strategy, I am much like C. S. Lewis, who described his conversion in *Surprised by Joy*. He called himself "the most dejected, reluctant convert in all of England…drug into the kingdom kicking, struggling, resentful, and darting his eyes in every direction for a chance of escape."[3]

The lure of the commodious room still echoes in my heart, but now a new voice challenges me in Southwest Florida to consider new ways to reach new people. It has called me to instead of domesticating or running off the APEs in our congregation to intentionally discover, develop, and deploy the APEs sitting in the chairs of our sanctuary. It lures me into deep, unknown waters to once again trust the Lord of the harvest for new people in very unique and new places.

So I am coming alongside Michael to share a few thoughts and tell a few stories about my missional experiences as a local church pastor and

---

2. *Journal of John Wesley,* June 23, 1759.

3. C. S. Lewis, *Surprised by Joy.*

leader. Together, we hope to awaken the Body and Bride of Jesus, especially in North America and Europe, to join Jesus in the "fields," which are described as "ripe for harvest" (John 4:35 NLT).

Jorge Acevedo
Lead Pastor
Grace Church
egracechurch.com

Framing

The Methodist movement was born in the *field*. John Wesley and those first Methodists joined what the Holy Spirit was up to in the fields with people who largely had no relationship with the church. Once again, the Spirit is up to something out in the fields with the "nones" (people who claim no religious affiliation or practice) and "dones" (people who once practiced a religion, but no longer do) of our post-everything society. While Fresh Expressions is an ecumenical movement with churches across the theological spectrum, it is also the most Methodist thing in the world today. So this book is a practical "field guide," live from the fields where a new Methodism is springing up from the ground.

This book is the result of the double-listening we encourage in fresh expressions—tuning our ears to both God and culture. For two thousand years, followers of Jesus have embodied and communicated the essential truths and practices revealed through scripture, refreshing the old signs in new ways for new contexts.

Menu: Rather than a table of "Contents," this book has a "Menu." Contents are *something contained, the subjects or topics covered in a book or document with chapters or other formal divisions of a book or document.* I offer, instead, a menu, which is *a list of options, especially one displayed on a screen, or the food available to be served in a restaurant or at a meal.*

Rather than content to be mastered, fresh expressions are a series of delicious meal options, which you can chose to engage or not. This collection of learnings may provide one idea, one image, one story, which may spark new life in communities and congregations. A meal is a provisional offering; it only stays warm or fresh for a period of time. In a rapidly shifting age, when what tomorrow holds is quite uncertain, we can only share recipes and gather at table one day at a time. We prefer even more for you to think of sitting down together for the most Methodist phenomenon of all... the potluck! Survey the various options and choose to partake of what seems the most mouthwatering.

Movement: There's no "Introduction" here, rather a "Movement." In former days, the church provided foundational narratives—the stories that shaped societies which were part of Christendom. Today, these archetypal stories appear primarily on screens (movie screens, phone screens, and flat screens). Good stories grab you with a movement, a cinematic technique that scans the vista to show what's coming. This movement pans across the fields of Methodism, then and now, serving as the "why" of this book, a vision of what you can expect and an introduction to some key concepts.

Downloads: Rather than chapters, this book has downloads. A chapter is *the main division of a book, typically with a number or title.* Or a chapter can be *the governing body of a religious community, especially a cathedral or a knightly order.* Downloads are a more transparent reflection of what we are offering. These downloads came through prayer, meditation, engaging scripture, conversation, experience, and research. A download is *the act or process of downloading data.* We downloaded this data from a wide variety of church experience, and now we're curating it as a gift for you to download. You are encouraged to digest it, transform it, and offer it to others for download.

Remix simply means to mix again, or to create a new version by recombining and re-editing the elements of the existing versions. Approximately midway through each download I will offer a "remix." We will look at the beliefs and practices of early Methodism, then show how the Spirit is remixing them for the new missional frontier through the Fresh

Expressions movement today. Following each download will be a series of "Field Stories."

Field Stories are evidence that "vile" Methodists are still taking it to the fields today through this movement that we call "fresh expressions." I will collect and share these field stories with you to demonstrate how the concepts I discuss are being lived out today on the new missional frontier. Planting new churches or initiating ministries among new people, in the wild, involves failure. Innovation is an iterative process that involves experimentation and learning from failure. The entire human journey is really one of failing forward. The Methodist movement has been marked by failure, improvisation, and adaptation. Every successful fresh expression of church is built on the back of learning from failures. I will share some of our most epic ones with you here as well.

Missional Field Kits follow the Field Stories as a series of suggested exercises, tools, or discussion questions to try with your team. We envision them as "kits" you can open up and use in your fields.

Missiographies: John Wesley harnessed the power of the emerging print technology of his day in the regular publication of select journal articles. These were an expanded narrative of his own spiritual journey (autobiographical), used strategically to fuel the movement under his care (missional). This is something Jorge Acevedo has done exceptionally well throughout his ministry through the emerging technologies of our time (social media, websites, and cellular communications). Each Download will conclude with a "missiography" from Jorge.

Credits are the culmination of the work of many beautiful minds. This reference section makes this book more credible.

Alternate Endings are sometimes included in great films. If you read all the way past the credits, there may be something special in store! Can your church experience an alternate ending?

Movement

A Vile Movement Begins in the Fields

The "Holy Club" of Christ Church, Oxford University, began with a handful of men derogatively called "Methodists" by their peers in 1729. Near the time of John Wesley's death in 1791, a growing percentage of English women and men had become Methodist. In 1776, an upstart nation called America boasted a population in which fewer than 2 percent of people were Methodists. By 1850, over 34 percent of the population had joined the Methodist movement.[1] Wesley scholar Paul Chilcote, using records from the first and foundational Conference Journals, shows that the ratio of Methodists to general US population in 1773 was around 1:2000, whereas by 1784 it was around 1:200.[2]

How did this happen? What can we learn? Where did it all begin? Is a remixed Methodism emerging again today? If so, how do we join into what God is up to?

It all started in a *field*—with a people willing to be *vile*.

Movements may be impregnated in the heat of a heart strangely warmed, but the delivery room is the fields. A heart set on fire with the

---

1. Steve Addison, estimates near the time of Wesley's death "one in thirty English men and women were Methodist," quoted in Alan Hirsch, *The Forgotten Ways: Reactivating the Missional Church* (Grand Rapids, MI: Zondervan, 2006), 20.

2. Paul Chilcote, from presentations in United Methodist History courses taught at Asbury Theological Seminary.

love of God cannot contain the flames. That flaming love must be shared or the recipient risks spontaneous combustion. Furthermore, a person who has tasted that love does not schedule an appointed time and place, then sit back and wait for others to come receive it. He or she goes to others where they are and pours it out profusely in the same manner it was received. This love can send us to people and places that the privileged society deems "vile." This love of God among ordinary people awakened a movement in the fields, and it's happening again in the Fresh Expressions movement.

The *fields* are a metaphor for the places where the people are, where they gather and share life. The field represents vulnerability and the humility to enter the unknown—to go empty handed into a space where we don't have all the answers.

The spiritual fire that awakened John Wesley's heart at Aldersgate was unleashed in a field just outside of Bristol, England. A heart aflame with God's love can ignite a revolution in the fields, *when we find a contextually appropriate expression for its embodiment.*

We hope God will "make Methodism *vile* again." People are often confused when we speak like this. Perhaps it is peculiar to ponder how the Fresh Expressions movement, alongside existing congregations, helps Methodists awaken to our missional DNA and heritage as a "vile" renewal movement. Folks often look puzzled and say, "you mean *vital again*, right?" No, we actually mean "vile." In fact, most local churches will never truly be able to become more *vital* unless they are first willing to become more *vile*.

We also don't soften the word *vile*; we mean it in the denotive sense, as in extremely unpleasant, foul, nasty, unsavory, utterly repulsive, of little worth or value, and so on. We also have chosen to use the word *Methodist* because it was the reluctant title that John Wesley accepted for himself and the people involved in the movement he catalyzed. However, we mean that broader umbrella that includes all followers of Jesus in the Wesleyan tradition, and further, all the missional renegades in every various expression of the church.

We are also aware of the danger of using the language of making anything great, vile, or glorious "again." This is a statement that smacks of "presentism," the uncritical hubris of seeing one's own time and intelligence as superior to all that precedes, or the mindless adherence to the dominant *zeitgeist*, especially the tendency to interpret past events through our post-everything lens. Of the many "isms" of our society, racism, sexism, nationalism, and alcoholism . . . presentism is surely one of the most prevalent.

At the same time, followers of Jesus are a peculiar people, for our future is in our past. Life starts in the garden of creation, walking with God in the cool of the day (Gen 3:8 NIV). Life starts again in a garden of flower-covered graves—a cemetery with an empty tomb—where the death conquering master of all is mistaken for the gardener or undertaker (John 20:15). Life continues eternally in an urban garden where we once again gather at the tree of life (Rev 22:1-5). Our future is a remix of our past, breaking into the present. The scriptures teach us to "remember" again and again. To remember what God has done, to understand our past, to learn from it, to understand how it shapes our future. There is indeed something great about Methodism that needs to be recovered, and we believe it's the vileness of *being church in the fields*.

John Wesley observed that the Anglican Church that he loved and served was largely failing to reach the masses of people in his day. In the eighteenth century, there was a great gulf between the wealthy minority and the immobilized masses experiencing poverty. It was a time of enormous social and economic change and dislocation that included massive population growth as well as urbanization. The Industrial Revolution was dawning, and the seeds of a global economy were being planted.

The Enlightenment created a wave of clergy who embraced the assumptions of Deism. In the drive to create a religion of pure rationality, Christianity was reduced to a system of moral precepts. The scriptures were considered crude, inconsistent, and even immoral. Belief in the Trinity, incarnation, special revelation, and miracles were criticized and dismissed. A kind of enlightened clergy caste system was formed. The church was regarded with suspicion and deep skepticism.[3]

Wesley and his band of vile ones saw a growing disconnect between the church and the people the church was supposed to be reaching. There was a sense that the episcopal bureaucracy of his day had become rigid, unyielding, and lifeless. Wesley's passion to connect with people outside the reach of the current structure of the church drove him to embrace some of the emerging missional innovations.

Wesley biographer Albert Outler suggested that we tend to overemphasize Wesley's "heart strangely warmed" experience at Aldersgate. He showed from Wesley's own journal that this awakening was the culmination of a series of significant moments, followed by "further crises of equal, or nearly equal" impact.[4] Yes, it was a crucial moment along Wesley's spiritual journey, when his intellectual convictions were transformed by personal experience, but we have tended to the extremes of overvaluing or undervaluing what preceded and what followed.

The Holy Club the Wesley brothers formed at Oxford to pursue a sanctified life (1720–1735) was later described by Wesley as the "first rise of Methodism." The Moravians singing joyfully in the storms at sea while Wesley himself was gripped with fear in 1735 on the way to Georgia, and the failed missionary activities in the American colonies, was the "second rise of Methodism" (1736–1738). This led up to the "heart strangely warmed" conversion that happened at Aldersgate Street in London on May 24, 1738, the forming of the Fetter Lane Society, and the "third rise of Methodism."[5]

3. Stephen Sykes, John E. Booty, and Jonathan Knight, *The Study of Anglicanism* (London, UK: SPCK/Fortress, 1998), 32–33.

4. Albert C. Outler, ed., *John Wesley* (New York: Oxford University Press, 1964), 52.

5. Paul W. Chilcote, *Recapturing the Wesleys' Vision: An Introduction to the Faith of John and Charles Wesley* (Woodstock, VT: Skylight Paths Publishing, 2011), 6–7.

However, a close reading of his journal conveys that Wesley still struggled spiritually following the Aldersgate experience. More and more churches began to close their doors to Wesley. He personally struggled with both his *ordinary* call, which came through episcopal ordination, and the seeming pull toward an *extraordinary* call to those currently unreached by the parish system. Wesley biographer Arthur Skevington Wood describes the latter as a calling to be "missioner extraordinary to the lost sheep of the land."[6]

It wasn't until all those experiences found embodied expression in a revolutionary new way that a true transformation occurred, and the Methodists became a distinct swell in the larger wave of the Evangelical Revival. The passion to serve those deemed "vile" by society, the sick, poor, and imprisoned started in the Holy Club at Oxford. Yet that passion drove John Wesley throughout his life and ministry. Wood wrote, "The hungry multitude looked up for someone to feed them with spiritual bread. Here was his constituency, but as yet he had to be introduced to *a means of reaching it*"[7] (italics mine).

On April 2, 1739, at the compulsion of his friend George Whitefield, John Wesley went to a field just outside what was then the city limits of Bristol, England. Bristol was a city of approximately 50,000 people, an emerging hub of commercial activity. It was an important port for trade with North America and the West Indies, exporting manufactured goods, and reprehensibly, African slaves. What's truly noteworthy for our discussion is that Bristol was surrounded by the coal mines that would help fuel the dawning Industrial Age.[8]

There, among the coal miners who would transform the structure of society through their sweat and groaning backs, Wesley tried this missional innovation called field preaching. About three thousand people

---

6. Arthur S. Wood, *The Burning Heart: John Wesley, Evangelist* (Minneapolis: Bethany Fellowship, 1978), 76.

7. Wood, *The Burning Heart,* 70.

8. Richard P. Heitzenrater, *Wesley and the People Called Methodists* (Nashville: Abingdon Press, 1995), 98.

showed up, many of whom had no connection with a church. Later Wesley wrote in his journal, "At four in the afternoon I submitted to be more vile and proclaimed in the highways the glad tidings of salvation...."[9] Outler carefully examines Wesley's journals and writes of this experience,

> It is most impressive to observe the marked effect this success at Bristol had on Wesley's spiritual equilibrium. Up to this point the story is full of anxiety, insecurity, futility. Hereafter, the instances of spiritual disturbances drop off sharply and rarely recur, even in the records of a very candid man.[10]

Chilcote describes this moment as the "genuine birth of the Methodist revival."[11] In open-air preaching, Wesley found his *channel of communication*, the *means* to reach his constituency. John crossed the threshold of his true vocation not in a parish church, a university classroom, or a prayer meeting, but in the *field*:

> Too many obstacles were placed in his path. He could now turn to the unchurched multitudes and meet them on their own ground with an unsullied conscience.[12]... He was the chosen apostle of the masses. But before he could reach his divinely appointed constituency, a way of approach had to be found. Traditional methods would never succeed in touching the thousands outside the churches. A new means of contact was needed. It was provided by open air preaching....Being excluded from the churches he was driven into the fields. Henceforward his was to be a predominately extra-mural ministry.[13]

We lose the radical nature of this endeavor in our modern context. For most of the clergy and church-goers of Wesley's day, field preaching was unacceptable. John himself resisted it: "I could scarce reconcile myself at first to this *strange way* of preaching in the fields... having been all my

---

9. Heitzenrater, *Wesley and the People Called Methodists*, 99.

10. Outler, *John Wesley*, 17.

11. Chilcote, *Recapturing the Wesleys' Vision*, 8.

12. Wood, *The Burning Heart*, 89

13. Wood, *The Burning Heart*, 83.

life (till very lately) so tenacious of every point relating to decency and order, that I should have thought the *saving* of souls *almost a sin* if it had not been done *in a church*."[14] Even John's elder brother Samuel criticized him and wrote to their mother Susanna of his concerns with John's field preaching.

Wesley's willingness "to face rejection and even hostility from others" and "relinquishment of religious respectability" is an often-neglected aspect of Wesley's ministry.[15]

For an example, consider one of Wesley's critics, Joseph Trapp:

> For a clergyman of the Church of England to pray and preach in the fields, in the country, or in the streets of the city, is perfectly new, a fresh honour to the blessed age in which we have the happiness to live. I am ashamed to speak on a subject which is a reproach not only to our Church and country but to human nature itself. Can it promote Christianity to turn into riot, tumult, and confusion? To make it ridiculous and contemptible, and to expose it to the scorn and scoffs of infidels and atheists? To the prevalence of immorality and profaneness, infidelity and atheism, is now added the pest of enthusiasm. Our prospect is very sad and melancholy. Go not after these imposters and seducers; but shun them as you would the plague.[16]

Despite the derision of his many critics, most of whom were clergymen, Wesley took up this vile practice of field preaching and, borrowing from similar practices of his day, designed an apostolic discipleship process. Wesley reached the people who were not connecting with the established church, taking the gospel to the fields, miners' camps, and debtors' prisons. He connected new believers whose only entrance requirement for membership in the societies was a "desire to flee the wrath to come," to small gatherings of people who journeyed on in the life of grace together (societies, classes, bands).

---

14. John Wesley, et al., *The Works of John Wesley* (Nashville: Abingdon Press, 1984), 2:167.

15. Seamands, quoted in Paul W. Chilcote, *The Wesleyan Tradition: A Paradigm for Renewal* (Nashville: Abingdon Press, 2002), 125.

16. Wood, *The Burning Heart*, 96.

Aside from the well-known accusations of "enthusiasm," a focus on personal testimonies of conversion, and the boisterous nature of the early "shouting Methodists," Wesley did other "vile" things. He assembled, trained, deployed, and oversaw a small army of lay preachers. These itinerant Methodist circuit riders and local leaders did not have the proper Anglican credentials, and they often invaded the parish territory of the ordained priests. One key in early Methodism's success was the unflinching tenacity of these "lay preachers." This was an awakening of the "priesthood of all believers" (apostles, prophets, evangelists, shepherds, teachers)—the whole people of God.[17]

And yet there was more vileness in addition to field preaching, lay preaching, extemporaneous prayer, and other "irregular" practices. Not only did Wesley encourage women to lead the Methodist societies; as the movement progressed they also joined the ranks of lay preachers. Perhaps this full inclusion of women was deeply influenced by Wesley's mother, Susanna, who pioneered the first "fresh expression" in her kitchen—a full "church service" that grew to include about two hundred participants.[18] Women led, preached, organized, and figured prominently in the movement from its genesis. This was not permissible in the established church of Wesley's day.[19]

Later there would be significant debate concerning the lay preachers serving sacraments, as well as charges of separatism. The Methodists became known as "rabble rousers," accused of being "big with mischief" in their "unauthorized gatherings" that disturbed the peace of post-Restoration England.[20] Wesley's messages were considered crude, and the "unaccustomed frankness" of his delivery was offensive to the sensibilities

---

17. Heitzenrater, *Wesley and the People Called Methodists*, 93.

18. Chilcote, *Recapturing the Wesleys' Vision*, 8.

19. Ryan N. Danker, *Wesley and the Anglicans: Political Division in Early Evangelicalism* (Downers Grove, IL: IVP Academic, 2016), 131.

20. Danker, *Wesley and the Anglicans*, 98.

of the learned minds of the Enlightenment.[21] The Methodist movement started in the fields, with the vile riff raff of the day. The crowds of the marginalized, the uneducated, and those experiencing poverty gathered by the tens of thousands to hear and respond to the gospel. Many became indigenous leaders in the movement.

It might be a stretch to call John Wesley an innovator, but like other innovators, he spotted cultural waves and drew from and enhanced practices that were emerging. Field preaching was already happening, and Wesley joined fellow "irregulars" like George Whitefield in this practice. German Pietists sought to renew the Lutheran Church by returning to traditional Reformation themes through creation of the *collegia pietatis* (colleges of piety) which were small groups gathered together for Bible study and prayer. An adaptation of these groups for the Church of England became the *religious societies* (started by Anthony Horneck in the 1670s). By the dawn of the eighteenth century, the societies movement birthed centralized organizations like the Society for Promoting Christian Knowledge (SPCK). John grew up in a home in which his father Samuel was involved in the SPCK, and John became a member himself later.[22] Furthermore, other groups, as part of the larger Evangelical Revival, prayed extemporaneously, utilized laity, took personal conversion seriously, sought to recover the primitive form of the church, and utilized print media culture to further their movements.

John's true genius was in his ability to weave these innovations together in a robust system that combined discipleship with ethics, while creating a relational network that would sustain the movement beyond his own influence. Perhaps he was more of an adaptor than an innovator—a master of the remix.

John Wesley was not a perfect man. We do not make him into an idol—though perhaps an icon—nor would he want us to. I've heard people refer to Wesley as a hallowed saint, womanizer, failed husband,

21. Wood, *The Burning Heart*, 285.

22. Heitzenrater, *Wesley and the People Called Methodists*, 19–21.

workaholic, and egomaniac. Like all human beings, he had issues. I see Wesley as a spiritual forebearer, and I seek to follow Jesus with as much passion and commitment as he did. Yet Wesley is not the key to missional engagement for our time. Wesley could not possibly foresee and offer prescriptions for the complexities of missional evangelism and social holiness in our day.

Further, there are some practices I advocate that John Wesley would hardly encourage, such as the "open table" as an altar call, the practices of tattooing, yoga, or people experiencing church in bars while consuming alcohol. However, you will grant there is more in the institutional versions of Methodism today that Wesley would not agree with, such as Holy Communion only once a month, pastors who run political campaigns to be elected bishop, the absence of field preaching, laity existing in a state of spiritual "learned helplessness" and completely dependent on professional clergy, or the lack of societies, classes, and bands, to name a few. Wesley himself literally forecasted that Methodism would be as good as dead if this ever became the case.

Instead I take the "first principles," the seeds of Wesley's organizing principles and practices, then replant them on the new missional frontier. For instance, the greatest "and" of the Methodist movement is rarely even recognized. John Wesley was a faithful Anglican priest until the day he died, *and* a missional renegade who preached in the fields. He sustained a tether back to the inherited church and encouraged people to participate fully in her life, and yet he said where church structures constrained the focus on missional evangelism, he "laid them aside."[23] He was a man who challenged the inherited system deeply, while trying to bring renewal to it. He held together competing ideas that divided believers in his day in creative tension. It is the seeds of *these ideas*, this *andness*, that we must plant in the fertile land that we inhabit. The seeds will grow into the shade of

23. *The Works of John Wesley,* Letters, Vol. II, "To 'John Smith,' 25 June, 1746" (Nashville: Abingdon Press, 1984), 77–78.

trees under which future generations of Christ-followers will sit, but they will grow in ways we will not expect either.

We follow the advice of our spiritual forefather: where we "might not think alike," with John Wesley, we will choose to "love alike" as he did. We will take his hand, in the places where our hearts are the same as his. We too will "set aside" the confining structures born from Wesley's own thought, to center ourselves in missional engagement for the emerging mission field of the present century. These risk-taking, system-bending practices in the pursuit of holiness make us the most "Wesleyan" of all.

Time for a Remix

Are you ready for déjà vu? Once again, a missional movement that began in the United Kingdom has found a home in the United States. Once again, the structures of society are engaged in massive transformation. Once again, much of the inherited church is not connecting with the larger population or engaging the culture in transformative ways. So an informal ecumenical group led primarily by Anglicans in the United Kingdom organized to create a report concerned with the continued decline of the church and the emergence of new ecclesial communities.

Let's make Methodism vile again! We offer you a *Field Guide to Methodist Fresh Expressions*.

The preface to the Declaration of Assent that all incoming Anglican clergy must confess says,

> The Church of England is part of the One, Holy, Catholic and Apostolic Church, worshipping the one true God, Father, Son and Holy Spirit. It professes the faith uniquely revealed in the Holy Scriptures and set forth in the catholic creeds, *which faith the Church is called upon to proclaim afresh in each generation* (italics mine).[24]

---

24. Graham Cray, *Mission-Shaped Church: Church Planting and Fresh Expressions in a Changing Context* (New York: Seabury, 2010), 100.

The phrase "Fresh Expressions" emerged from the conviction in this statement, with the team led by Bishop Graham Cray, who produced the *Mission-Shaped Church* (MSC) in 2004. The report became an international bestseller, is credited with transforming the ecclesiology of the Church of England, has catalyzed the development of thousands of fresh expressions, and released similar initiatives in Australia, Canada, mainland Europe, South Africa, the United States, and elsewhere.[25]

A fresh expression is a form of church for our changing culture, established primarily for the benefit of those who are not yet part of any church. These are forms of church that are

Missional: birthed by the Spirit to reach not-yet-Christians.

Contextual: seek to serve the context in an appropriate form to the people in it.

Formational: focused on making disciples.

Ecclesial: a full expression of the "church," not a stepping-stone to an inherited congregation.

The *Mission-Shaped Church* showed incredible insight to recognize the massive shift in the structure of society and the need for new forms of church. As Cray put it, "The Western world, at the start of the third millennium, is best described as a 'network society.' This is a fundamental change, 'the emergence of a new social order.'"[26]

Pioneering sociologist Manuel Castells posits that at the end of the second millennium, a new form of society arose from the interactions of several major social, technological, economic, and cultural transformations: the network society. We are currently now in a period of historical transition between different forms of society, moving from the Industrial Age into the Information Age. The network society consists of a social

---

25. Michael Moynagh, *Church in Life: Emergence, Ecclesiology and Entrepreneurship* (London, UK: SCM Press, 2017), 2.

26. Cray, *Mission-Shaped Church*, 4.

structure made up of networks enabled by microelectronics-based information and communications technologies.[27]

The "fields" have changed, as we will see through an examination of the "space of flows" and the "space of places" in a network society (*flows* are the means through which people, objects, and information are moved through social space). Multiple layers of networks, digital and physical, intertwine, connecting people in nodes and hubs, which we will explore as the first, second, and third places of local communities. These are the new "fields" of the Information Age.

Fresh Expressions are a powerfully effective way to engage this emerging societal milieu. The *Mission-Shaped Church* team didn't initiate the Fresh Expressions movement. They observed how the Holy Spirit was reaching not-yet-Christians and forming disciples of Jesus Christ where they already shared life. They provided language and began seeking to understand the movemental process of something God was initiating. By realizing the Holy Spirit was once again up to something out in the fields, the *Mission-Shaped Church* team "submitted to be more vile." They ultimately helped birth a cross-denominational movement, tethered to and alongside the institutional church.

Alan Hirsch and Dave Ferguson note that every historical renewal movement, among which they include early Methodism, recovers some degree of the following movemental elements: priesthood of believers, "kingdom of God" over "church," prophetic protest, church planting, or mission on the fringes and among the poor.[28] Indeed as we will see, early Methodism included each of these elements in a strong way. It seems that these missional waves of the Spirit are always breaking on the shore of history. There have been many of these waves, of which Methodism is only one. Fresh Expressions is early Methodism. . . remixed!

---

27. Manuel Castells, *The Rise of the Network Society* (Oxford and Malden, MA: Blackwell, 2000), xvii–xviii.

28. Alan Hirsch and Dave Ferguson, *On the Verge: A Journey into the Apostolic Future of the Church* (Grand Rapids, MI: Zondervan, 2011), 35.

The Fresh Expressions movement in the United States is emerging before our eyes in real time. We are paying attention to what the Holy Spirit is up to. Now we have new processes, language, and resources to join in. Fresh Expressions US has been a key instrument to catalyze this movement. Entire conferences, denominations, dioceses, networks, and beyond are catching on, embracing the movement, and entering into partnerships.[29] We are catching this wave of the Spirit together!

I serve as the Cultivator of Fresh Expressions in the Florida Conference of The United Methodist Church, and was the first clergy person appointed to this new role in the United States. Florida was the first conference to enter into a formal partnership with Fresh Expressions US. I live in a state where most congregations are in decline, less than 18 percent of the population is in worship on the weekend, and churches across the denominational spectrum close their doors every year. Our Bishop, Ken Carter, set forth a goal of five hundred fresh expressions of church by 2025.[30] Now, alongside over six hundred legacy congregations, over three hundred fresh expressions of church have emerged.

God's way of making "all things new" is not the same as our infatuation with brand-newness and wasted messaging. God takes the existing material and reworks it. Like a potter at the wheel, God takes what's marred and makes something new. God takes fragmented lives and reworks them into a mosaic of grace. Resurrection is about taking what's dead and decaying, and through a marvelous work of renewal making it eternally alive again. God is in the process of making the entire cosmos new in this way (Rom 8:18-23).

H. Richard Niebuhr once said, "The great Christian revolutions came not by the discovery of something that was not known before. They happen when someone takes radically something that was already there."

---

29. Chris Backert, https://freshexpressionsus.org/2018/12/10/fresh-expressions-us-year-end-review-2018/.

30. Ken Carter, "Church Vitality," https://www.flumc.org/church-vitality.

There is no "golden age" to which we should return. Before us now is an adaptive challenge. No amount of applying technical solutions to technical problems will reverse the decline.

The Fresh Expressions movement is not the next newfangled thing a bishop is asking us to try. This is a movement of the Holy Spirit, a new iteration of Methodists taking it to the fields again. It enables us to be church with people who will never come to our Sunday morning services and yet continue to serve the people who will. It is an awakening of the core identity of who we are as the people called Methodists. It is not in competition with your traditional activities as a congregation; it is a complement.

Furthermore, it's not only for large churches with staff and resources. In fact, we bring two different perspectives from this movement. Jorge, serving as lead pastor of a large, multi-site congregation, is launching fresh expressions across a whole region. I (Michael) am serving as a co-pastor of a revitalization congregation that had dwindled down to a handful of people.

Both Grace Church and Wildwood United Methodist Church have now become models of the "mixed economy" or "blended ecology" way. The *mixed economy* refers to a diversity of ecclesial forms in which fresh expressions of church exist alongside inherited forms in relationships of mutual respect and support.[31] The *blended ecology* refers to fresh expressions of church in symbiotic relationship with inherited forms of church in such a way that the combining of these modes over time merge to create a nascent form.[32]

Through fresh expressions not only are people being offered Christ for the first time, but inherited congregations are being revitalized by this approach. Joining into the *movementum* of fresh expressions allows existing churches to catch a fresh breath of resurrection. Both of our inherited

---

31. Michael Moynagh, *Being Church, Doing Life: Creating Gospel Communities Where Life Happens* (Grand Rapids, MI: Monarch, 2014), 432.

32. Michael Beck, *Deep Roots, Wild Branches: Revitalizing the Church in the Blended Ecology* (Franklin, TN: Seedbed, 2019).

congregations have experienced forms of revitalization through cultivating fresh expressions in our communities.

While some claim the Methodist movement traded our missional zeal for respectability, the Fresh Expressions movement is allowing us to make Methodism vile again. Institution and movement are beginning to operate together in a life-giving way. Can we learn to do so without once again exiling the very apostolic impulses that may give us life? Can we learn from our past mistakes to make possible a new future? Can we embrace both a neighborhood and a network approach to mission? Can we realign our systems to make room for pioneer ministry?

While the purpose of fresh expressions is to reach not-yet-Christians and be church with them where they are, churches that plant fresh expressions are experiencing revitalization. In other words, vileness leads to vitalness. We need to say right up front: this might not work at your church. You could integrate everything we share here in your congregation and it still might continue to decline and die. There are no secret ingredients or special sauces for church revitalization. We are concerned when advocates make such claims. However, we have both seen what God can do when local churches submit to be more vile and join what the Holy Spirit is up to in the fields.

We live out every day what we write about here. We are reporting from the fields, not from the church study. We simply love Jesus and his church; we have no other agenda. We share our learnings and failures to see renewal throughout the earth.

Jesus Is Lord of Neighborhoods and Networks

John Wesley understood the Methodist movement as a revival of primitive Christianity. He perceived a discontinuity between the church of his day and the early church. He loved the Anglican Church and gave his life toward her renewal. However, much of his activity was about returning to the first principles of scripture, which required significant missional adaptation. Methodism was a "renewal movement" within the larger church that was never intended to be separate from her. Wesley's "practical divinity" was centered in a rediscovery of the Bible, an awakening of the theology of the early church, lived out amidst the emerging missional opportunities of his day. Let's begin this journey by pondering the central claim of the early church, "Jesus is Lord" and how it's awakened in the fields.

The first Christians gathered around the confession of Jesus's Lordship, a title they believed was conferred on Jesus by God, based on the resurrection (Acts 2:32-36). After they saw Jesus resurrected bodily, they experienced him from then on, through the power of the Holy Spirit, as infinitely alive on both personal and communal levels (1 Cor 12:3). The Lordship of Jesus is a central theme of the New Testament, from the

1

prenatal confession in the womb of Mary (Luke 1:48) to the final benediction of John of Patmos in Revelation (Rev 22:20-21).

The early church's designation of Jesus as κύριος (*kyrios*)—Lord—was politically subversive in an empire where Caesar was declared Lord. Furthermore, the disciples worshipped Jesus as God, and this belief was passed down and articulated formally in 325 CE in the Nicene Creed, which clarifies Christ is "of one substance with the Father, begotten, not created."[1]

This personal relationship with the living Jesus, and allegiance to his Lordship was something that marked the early Methodist movement. The stories of personal experience and conversion were shared through the emerging print media of the day, helping to advance the Evangelical Revival. It was something seemingly absent in the institutional forms of the church and the clergy, whom Wesley frequently described as being Christians in name only.[2]

Historically, we have tried to grasp what this Lordship means by understanding it in "spheres." In the *personal sphere*, Jesus is Lord of the individual Christian. To say that Jesus is Lord means we put our whole faith and trust in him, surrender to his authority, and agree to let him be the ruler of our lives, one day at a time. In the *communal sphere*, Jesus is Lord of this community called the church—including local churches, denominations, and the universal church (Eph 5:23; Col 1:18).

That brings us to the *social sphere*—Jesus's Lordship is not limited to the church but encompasses all societies. All human claims to power are subject to Jesus. This assertion may seem at first glance like a conundrum in a world plagued with terrorist attacks, inequality, racism, poverty, and corruption at every level of most governments. One might ask, "How can Jesus be Lord of this?" One role of the church is to work among these fallen societies of the earth to bring the realization of Jesus's Lordship to

---

1. Henry S. Bettenson and Chris Maunder, *Documents of the Christian Church* (Oxford: Oxford University Press, 1999), 27.

2. Ryan N. Danker, *Wesley and the Anglicans: Political Division in Early Evangelicalism* (Downers Grove, IL: IVP Academic, 2016), 89.

bear. Indeed, Jesus and his followers have undeniably reshaped the societal sphere in incalculable ways for two thousand years.

This transformation has been a focus of Methodists since the Holy Club at Oxford. We practice both *personal holiness* and *social holiness*. We participate in works of piety that help us grow in love for God: prayer, studying scripture, worship, fasting, Holy Communion, and so on. We also expect our faith must be expressed in our works of mercy, that is, actions that seek justice and reconciliation for all people. In these ways, we seek to grow in love for our neighbor. Yet, we also realize that Jesus's reign has both future and present dimensions (Matt 13:33). From local mayors, to presidents and dictators, every human claim to power is hollow and ultimately accountable to Jesus (John 19:11; Phil 2:10-11). In the *cosmic sphere*, Jesus is Lord of the entire universe (Col 1:15-17).

Wesley is sometimes called a "folk theologian" who cobbled together the essential theological emphases of Continental Pietism and Eastern Orthodoxy into a "practical divinity." The previous (seventeenth) century saw regicide, socio-cultural upheaval, and the bloodshed of the English Civil War in which Christians killed each other in the name of the Prince of Peace. This was a scar on the living memory of the people, who in Wesley's day were in a time of national restoration. The age of the Industrial Revolution was dawning. Anything that threatened the *Pax Anglica* was highly suspect. The larger Evangelical Revival that Wesley influenced was a threat. There was in general an underlying deep skepticism of the church, and the activities of the first Methodists seemed to threaten what little emerging stability there was.

Wesley was significantly criticized by those who viewed the parish system as sufficient for reclaiming lost souls and making Christian converts in its current state. In defense of field preaching, Wesley wrote, "Therefore, it is evident that there are not churches enough. And one plain reason why, notwithstanding all these churches, they are no nearer being reclaimed, is this—they never come into a church, perhaps not once in a

3

twelve-month, perhaps not for many years together."[3] From Wesley's perspective, people were not coming "into a church" and the current parish system was insufficient for reaching the majority of people.

Furthermore, the Age of Enlightenment was creating a false dichotomy between faith and reason and moving society "forward" toward the latter in the name of progress. The emphasis of reason and scientific certainty penetrated the church and created a culture of detached Deism. A new protest from reason pushed against the Christian faith itself, and the first cracks resembling post-Christendom emerged. Wesley felt many clergy had abandoned the orthodox faith for enlightenment ideals.

Meanwhile, crime, alcoholism, and poverty plagued the general populace. Soldiers returning from the war between England and France joined the swell of marginalized masses, and they resorted to criminal activity. Wesley's strength was communicating the gospel in "plain words for plain people" with great urgency in the sore places and spaces where they did life. He also unleashed the "plain people," his army of lay preachers, to do it. In an ecclesial ecosystem in which the religious intelligentsia seemingly exchanged "Jesus is Lord" for "Reason is Lord," clergy were overeducated beyond their effectiveness. In many cases, they could no longer connect with the common people. Through small groups, and high expectations that all people would participate and grow as leaders, Wesley helped common people lay a thoughtful theological foundation for their lives.

We now have the great joy and challenge of ministering in a post-Christendom era in the United States. Emerging generations don't speak "Christianese" and typically have no life experience in the church. Therefore, to help people lay a theological foundation for their lives, we must learn to translate our practices into the emerging language of "plain words for plain people." Recovering our "practical divinity" requires comfortability with the "conjunctive" nature of Wesleyan theology, which is centered

---

3. John Wesley, et al., *The Works of John Wesley* (Nashville: Abingdon Press, 1984), Vol. VIII, p. 113. *A Farther Appeal to Men of Reason and Religion* (1745).

in a "both/and" mindset. Throughout this book we will see how differing perspectives can be held together in creative tension.[4]

Time for a Remix

It's time for a remix. Our "practical divinity" is fragile. Most churches in the Wesleyan tradition have given up the essential early practices that defined the movement. How regularly today are Methodists publicly accused of "irregularity," "innovation," "enthusiasm," and generally being "big with mischief" for stirring up the rabble in the fields? Have we traded in our narrative of a gutsy, boisterous movement for the narrative of the US corporation? Have we exchanged saddle sores and field preaching for white boards, board rooms, and PowerPoint presentations? The US corporate narrative was a perfect bedfellow for the church in a Christendom scenario in which the Eurotribal church enjoyed the privileged center of society. However, those corporate days are fading. We need the practices of the early Methodists, but they will take new forms on the frontier of a network society.

At the simplest level, a "network is a set of interconnected nodes."[5] So, these networks of technologically enabled flows of multimodal communication connect in real physical and digital localities that Castells calls "nodes." A node could be anything in a specific network, from a city, to a restaurant, to a park, to a laptop, to an iPhone screen. The nodes are the connection points determined by the network. For instance, the nodes of a financial network may be an automatically deposited paycheck in a banking site, an e-trade account on a home personal computer, a stock

---

4. Besides Outler, the conjunctive nature of Wesley's theology is highlighted by P. W. Chilcote who describes it as a "both/and" theology. (Paul W. Chilcote, *Recapturing the Wesleys' Vision: An Introduction to the Faith of John and Charles Wesley* [Woodstock, VT: Skylight Paths Publishing, 2011], 12). Will Willimon also affirms Wesleyan theology as "conjunctive theology" (*This We Believe: The Core of Wesleyan Faith and Practice* [Nashville: Abingdon Press, 2010], 31).

5. Manuel Castells, *The Rise of the Network Society* (Oxford and Malden, MA: Blackwell, 2000), 501.

market exchange, and the cash coming out of an ATM. The nodes of the illegal drug trade network that penetrates economies, states, and societies across the world could be "coca fields and poppy fields, clandestine laboratories, secret landing strips, street gangs, and money laundering financial institutions."[6]

So, what does this look like in our everyday lives? We most likely live in a place, our home, apartment, condominium, and so on. But our home is also a node in a larger network. We surf the web, Facetime, and send emails that have global implications at the speed of digital light. A friend through one of our social media sites (Facebook, Twitter, or Instagram, for example), invites us to a local coffee shop tomorrow afternoon. The coffee shop is a node where other networks interact. For instance, a yoga group is using the front porch, a group of entrepreneurs is convening in the back room, also connected here by the digitally enabled flows. (We will unpack the "space of flows" in the next Download.) The shop owner makes credit card transactions that travel as digital currency into the flows that connect a larger global financial network. Many networks are interacting in one location, all participating in a larger network of connections. Right at your local coffee shop!

In the liminality or "in-betweenness" of our time, as society itself moves through this fundamental change, we are transitioning into the post-industrial, knowledge-based era now described as the Information Age. One important aspect of this transformation as noted is *globalization*. Moynagh and Worsley define globalization simply as the world becoming "more interdependent and integrated," with physical, cultural, and virtual dimensions.[7] So technology has made the world smaller, and we are now a truly global community. Cultures consist of bundles of dynamic *practices*, connected across space and time through structured flows of information

---

6. Castells, *The Rise of the Network Society*, 501.

7. Michael Moynagh and Richard Worsley, *Going Global: Key Questions for the Twenty-First Century* (London, UK: A & C Black, 2008), 1–7.

and media.[8] Alan Hirsch describes practices as *embodiments of values.* This is the living out of a culture's assumptions in such a way that they can be observed and experienced by others.[9]

A typical week in the life of a person today involves spending most of the days on screens: phone screens, laptop screens, GPS screens, and flat screens. People may not know their own next-door neighbors but have a network of friends on social media that they meet with for face-to-face encounters to engage in practices together. Those practices could be a running group, yoga, or taking their kids to play sports. They could be centered upon a love for pets, or simply gathering at a favorite Mexican restaurant for burritos and beers.

The web and wireless communications are more than traditional media, they are a global means of interactive, multimodal, mass self-communication. Castells writes,

> For hundreds of millions of Internet users under 30, on-line communi-ties have become a fundamental dimension of everyday life that keeps growing everywhere...on-line communities are fast developing not as a virtual world, but as a real virtuality integrated with other forms of interaction in an increasingly hybridized everyday life.[10]

Thus, the distinction between real and virtual made by more chrono-logically mature generations is changing in the network society. Virtual reality is reality. Also, the idea of defining oneself by a locality is a fading phenomenon. Due to the power of mobilization and technologically en-abled flows, we may work in one city, go to school in another town, gather for communal practices in several cities, and yet live in another.

---

8. Ryan K. Bolger, "Practice Movements in Global Information Culture: Looking Back to McGavran and Finding a Way Forward," *Missiology* 35, no. 2: 181–93 (2007), 188.

9. Alan Hirsch and Dave Ferguson, *On the Verge: A Journey into the Apostolic Future of the Church* (Grand Rapids, MI: Zondervan, 2011), 174.

10. Castells, *The Rise of the Network Society*, xxix.

Len Sweet writes, "People today congregate not on shared streets but around shared interests."[11] Communities of practice are groups of people who share a common passion for an activity and grow in the performance of that practice as they interact regularly over time. The practice could be as complex as tattooing, or as simple as gathering for coffee, reading together at the library, or taking your dog to the dog park. Later I will discuss pioneer ministry. These pioneering Jesus followers live incarnationally in micro-communities gathering around a multitude of possible interests in a wide array of contextual variations. Within those practices, they, "through shared actions and words, point to the kingdom in such a way that the practice itself moves towards God."[12]

The missiological DNA of Donald McGavran has been rightly associated with the Fresh Expressions movement.[13] After thirty-two years on the mission field in India, McGavran wrote *The Bridges of God*. There he explains how "Peoples" become Christian rather than simply "individuals," which he sees as the primarily Western individualistic approach to Christianization. He describes layers or strata of society and how people are often confined within their own intimate stratum.[14] He argues that a people is not simply an aggregation of individuals but a "social organism." The attractional-only church mode (build it and they will come) can also be extractional, marked by personal conversion of the individual, followed by their removal from the social organism and placement in the new social organism: the "mission station" (for our purposes, the church compound).[15]

11. Leonard I. Sweet, *Me and We: God's New Social Gospel* (Nashville: Abingdon Press, 2014), 17.

12. Bolger, "Practice Movements in Global Information Culture," 189–90.

13. Louise Nelstrop and Martyn Percy, *Evaluating Fresh Expressions: Explorations in Emerging Church: Responses to the Changing Face of Ecclesiology in the Church of England* (Norwich: Canterbury Press, 2008), 38.

14. Donald A. McGavran, *The Bridges of God: A Study in the Strategy of Missions* (Eugene, OR: Wipf & Stock, 2005), 1.

15. McGavran, *The Bridges of God*, 8–11.

McGravran proposes that "extraction," removing someone from that social organism, is exactly the wrong thing to do. This does violence to the social organism and actually defeats the larger missional purpose. He notes a phenomenon called "group mind" in which individuals don't understand themselves as a self-sufficient unit but part of a group. Peoples are Christianized as this "group-mind is brought into a life-giving relationship to Jesus as Lord."[16]

Peoples become Christian through a chain reaction, a wave of decisions for Christ, sweeping through the group mind, which McGavran calls a "people movement." These groups are usually small in number, but through a series of small groups being instructed in the faith over a period of years, large numbers of new Christians can manifest.[17]

McGavran's missional approach has suffered major criticisms—particularly the Homogenous Unit Principle (HUP), which states that in subsections of society, members of those subsections who have some characteristics in common prefer to become Christians without crossing racial, linguistic, or class barriers.[18] However, missiologist Ryan Bolger reminds us that these critiques are more reflective of McGavran's American "translators" who, in the 1990s, hijacked and twisted his concepts to grow suburban mega-churches.[19] Later, I will explain the missional approach Bolger calls a "practice movement," which is McGavran's "people movement" remixed for a network society.

Vincent Donovan was a Roman Catholic priest who served as a missionary to the Masai people in Tanzania for seventeen years during the 1960s and 1970s. He also saw that the highly individualized Western approach of evangelizing people one by one is ineffective. Donovan too struggled with what he saw as an "extractional" approach. He saw that the dominant missional paradigm created communities of outcasts, now

---

16. McGavran, *The Bridges of God*, 8–11.

17. McGavran, *The Bridges of God*, 12–13.

18. Nelstrop and Percy, *Evaluating Fresh Expressions*, 38.

19. Bolger, "Practice Movements in Global Information Culture," 182.

dependent on the church and unable to impact their social group. Typically, *communities* of people become Christian or they don't at all. Donovan's evangelistic efforts among the Masai demonstrated that people are indeed converted at the level of a homogenous unit.[20]

Fresh expressions form among groups of people who are a "workable community," often connected by some ritual, place, or hobby. These are living social organisms distinct from other social groups. A fundamental premise of the missional church movement is not to extract people from their indigenous communities and bring them back to the church compound for proper Christianization but to help those communities form church where they are. This enables the church, largely inaccessible to many, to manifest in every nook and cranny of everyday life.

Paul Chilcote writes that the Wesleys in their own day rediscovered what we would call today this "missional church."[21] Wesley became an incarnational presence in the fields, boldly proclaiming the Lordship of Jesus, and inviting hearers to join into that reign. Groups of people for whom the church was largely inaccessible became Christian communities. Today, pioneers incarnate themselves in the new "fields" (the nodes of a network society), and through a loving, relational, *witness* approach to evangelism, invite communities of people to live together under the Lordship of Jesus.

In a network society, while we are hyper-connected all the time, never have we been more alone. Isolation is the great soul wound of our time. Fresh expressions of church form organically with groups of people connecting in neutral places around shared practices. The practice itself will be transformed as the disciple seeks to live under the Lordship of Jesus in the micro-community. Other participants in that practice can experience transformation as they grow in their relationship with the Jesus follower. Conversion is less about praying a sinner's prayer and more about obeying the Spirit nudges that occur through the messy relational process around

---

20. Vincent J. Donovan, *Christianity Rediscovered* (Maryknoll, NY: Orbis, 2003), 64.

21. Chilcote, *Recapturing the Wesleys' Vision*, 20.

the shared practice. The healing from isolation is a mutual exchange between the disciple and the not-yet-Christian. Contextual churches form, native to that community of practice, as Christians and not-yet-Christians live together in friendship and form a common language. The Holy Spirit is transforming the dispositions of the participants through the waves of grace as they enter more fully into Jesus's Lordship together.

The emergence of this new form of society necessitates a revolution in the missionary approach in the United States. How is Jesus Lord of the network society? How can we be a church not only for our neighborhoods but also for our networks? John Wesley saw the change in his own day, and adapted practices to reach people where they were. This is what the Fresh Expressions movement is allowing us to do today: planting churches or new networked ministries in the wild, with new people, in new places, and in new ways.

We need vintage forms of church to engage our neighborhoods *and* fresh forms of church to engage the networks all around us. Further, one professional clergy person doing the work of evangelism to grow his or her flock is a bankrupt concept. The new missional frontier requires the whole people of God, the "priesthood of all believers." Every Christian may invite others in their relational sphere to live under the Lordship of Jesus. Pioneers are a new breed of "lay preachers" turning their interest and hobbies into forms of church. A new movement of the "common people" is being unleashed.

Field Story—Beck

To be the church in the fields again, we need to recover an emphasis on a personal conversion experience, which means sharing that conversion testimony publicly. Will Willimon notes one of the keys to the success of the early Methodist movement was an emphasis on a distinct experience of God's love that is personal, convincing, and transforming.[22] We are also

---

22. Will Willimon, *Why I Am a United Methodist* (Nashville: Abingdon Press, 1990), 19.

discovering that emerging generations long to see authenticity and leaders who are transparent about their past and present struggles. I'll start by sharing my own experience of how Jesus redeemed me from a broken life in the shambles of failure.

In my earliest memories, I am sitting beside my grandmother, front pew on the preacher's right, at St. Mark's United Methodist Church in Ocala, Florida (hereafter referred to as St. Mark's). In those first formative years of my life, I stood with those precious folks and recited, "I believe in Jesus Christ, his only Son, *our Lord....* I believe in the *Holy Spirit*"[23] (emphasis mine). I confessed those words with my mouth, but believing them in my heart has been a long journey (Rom 10:9-10). Looking back now, I understand that even then the Holy Spirit was at work in prevenient ways. Pastor Holland Vaughn and the people of St. Mark's gathered around me at my infant baptism. Together they took responsibility to surround me with "a community of love and forgiveness" and to raise me to know Jesus as my Lord.[24] They stepped into the gap of loss in my life when I was an orphan. They fed me through their never-ending potlucks and loved me into the reality of Jesus's Lordship.

Nevertheless, I turned away and brought devastating consequences upon myself. Alcohol mastered me. I failed God, myself, and my family. I burned every bridge and broke every good thing God had placed in my life. I tasted God's goodness and turned away in shame. This earthquake of continuous failure landed me on a jailhouse floor. It was there that Jesus came into my life. In that vile place, I felt the warmth of his love and forgiveness in my heart. Today Jesus is my Lord, he is my master, I belong to him, my life is dependent on him.

Jesus recovered me in a vile place, a "field" far away from a church steeple. His love set my heart on fire in the confinement of that cell. That's partly why I cannot wait back on the altar of sparsely populated pews of

---

23. *The United Methodist Hymnal: Book of United Methodist Worship* (Nashville: United Methodist Publishing House, 1989), no. 881.

24. *United Methodist Hymnal*, 40.

the congregations I serve. That's why we go to the fields. In my case, that looks like having church in the tattoo parlor, the dog park, the Martin Luther King Jr. Building, the Mexican restaurant, and the yoga studio. It was from that place of deep failure that I became willing to unlearn everything I thought I knew and relearn how to live. Confined in a jail cell, going through withdrawal, and in the ashes of failure, I experienced freedom for the first time in my life.

Perhaps this is why my favorite Methodist hymn remains "And Can It Be," particularly the verse that captures my failure story...

> Long my imprisoned spirit lay
> Fast bound in sin and nature's night;
> Thine eye diffused a quickening ray,
> I woke, the dungeon flamed with light;
> My chains fell off, my heart was free,
> I rose, went forth, and followed Thee.
> My chains fell off, my heart was free,
> I rose, went forth, and followed Thee.[25]

As a pastor, I have served small rural churches, midsized revitalization congregations, and as an associate pastor at one of the fastest growing Methodist mega-churches in the United States.

Throughout my ministry, I have seen individuals accept Jesus's Lordship in both subtle and dramatic ways. Some of our most faithful and devoted leaders are baptized as infants and quietly grow lifelong into accepting that Lordship. I believe this is such a wonderful and valid way to live under the rule of Jesus.

However, in a post-Christian context, these folks seemingly are rare. So I must confess my passion for those who encounter Christ in palpably transformative ways. In those moments, you can literally see the change of Lordship. Wildwood United Methodist Church (hereafter Wildwood), was a church experiencing decades of decline that had dwindled down to

25. *United Methodist Hymnal,* "And Can It Be That I Should Gain," no. 363.

about thirty in worship. We have received hundreds of new members in the eight years I've been appointed there. Most of these had their initial interaction with our church not in the sanctuary but in our fresh expressions of church meeting throughout the community. Yet, some visit our traditional congregation because they hear about our fresh expressions. Usually they come by profession of faith, brand new Christians, coming to Christ in dramatic ways.

Mojo walked into the 11 a.m. worship experience with his family. An imposing figure, Mojo was literally covered with tattoos. As a tattoo artist, he heard about Tattoo Parlor Church, one of the fresh expressions of our blended ecology church. He found it intriguing that Christians would go into tattoo shops, study the Bible, get faith-based tattoos, and participate in the Lord's Supper. When we concluded worship with our weekly offering of Holy Communion, Mojo was on his knees at the altar rail, sobbing. Once the congregation processed out of the sanctuary, I joined Mojo at the altar. Still on his knees, I put my arms around him, and we wept together as he confessed his sins and asked for help. Mojo broke free that day from the tyranny of jails, institutions, and death. He began his life anew under the Lordship of Jesus.

Mojo was drawn into the "communal sphere" by the very nature of his baptism and personal allegiance to Jesus. He discovered that one cannot be a Christian in isolation; he now belongs to this "community of love and forgiveness" called the church. Our church has nurtured Mojo on his journey of grace, identified his gifts, and now, as he pursues ministry, we are sending him in mission.

Because of Mojo and other "field preachers" like him, we are powerfully impacting the local community and society at large. Mojo is a consummate evangelist who has offered Christ to many at his job site, incarnating God's love in the neighborhoods and networks of his daily interactions. Each life that he invites under the rule of Jesus has the potential of reaching more lives. Hence, Mojo is now causing ripples in eternity as he dedicates himself to God's redemptive mission to the cosmos, of which "Jesus is Lord."

Missiography—My Calling (Acevedo)

I received my call to ministry while sitting in the top row of a physics class at Valencia Community College in Orlando, Florida. I had become a follower of Jesus two years earlier and six months later landed in Pine Castle United Methodist Church, a mainline church going through charismatic renewal. Charismatic renewal in a mainline church in the late 1970s meant after singing a few gospel hymns, we sang a couple of Maranatha Music choruses and lifted our hands in worship. At that time, Jesus, faith, and the church were new to me.

I had wanted to be an architect, thus I was in the physics class. As the professor lectured, my mind drifted and a thought registered in my brain. "What brings you joy?" the Voice asked. I responded, "Helping teach the junior high Sunday school class." I'm not sure what happened, but with that response a new resolve gripped me. So I stood up, gathered my books, and thirty minutes later, I was in the office of the Reverend Clarence Yates. I shared with Pastor Yates my physics class experience and asked him, "What happened to me?" I had been in a local church for eighteen months, and truth be told, I loved Jesus and marijuana, God and girls. I was not ready for the cover of *Christianity Today*. Pastor Yates responded to my question with "Jorge, I think God is calling you into ministry." My unformed Christian mind had no category for "God is calling you into ministry." "What's that?" I naively retorted. "Well, it's doing the kind of stuff I do," my kind and wise pastor said. "Yes! I want to do that."

Within a few weeks, I bought a red cardboard footlocker from K-Mart for all my worldly goods. I flew to Kentucky and at Asbury College I began the third year of my freshman year.

But before flying eight hundred and fifty miles away to follow this thing called "God's calling," I needed to meet with my not-yet-Christian

15

parents to break the news to them. With a twenty-five-year career as an enlisted man in the United States Air Force behind him, my Dad had hoped I'd be an officer and a fighter pilot. Mom just wanted me to get a degree and a good job.

As we sat across the kitchen table from each other, I told the story of my calling during physics class and my meeting with Pastor Yates. They had both been intrigued at my new-found faith. Dad said, "If you're going to do this, then you cannot take your car." Now there were two things I loved at the ripe old age of twenty: Jesus and my 1976 Chevy Camaro. It was candy-apple red with a three-hundred-fifty-four barrel in it, a cassette player, and six-by-nine-inch coaxial speakers in back. She was my baby. Without thinking, I reached in my pocket and pulled out my keys, sliding them across the table to my Dad and said, "I've got to follow Jesus."

Weeks later, I flew to and enrolled at Asbury College in Wilmore, Kentucky, having declared myself a Bible major. I figured if I was going to be a pastor, I'd need to know the Bible. I lived in Trustees Main dormitory, and one evening early that first fall quarter, a group of guys from my dorm and I were sitting on the front stoop. Frankly, there was not much to do in the thriving metropolis of Wilmore, Kentucky. Front stoop conversations helped pass the time. "What do you want to do when you finish here?" was the question of the evening. "I want to be a teacher," one said. "I'm going to be a missionary to Africa," another replied. We went around the circle and they got to me. Naively, I said with great boldness, "I want to change the world for Jesus!" And they laughed, but I meant it.

Almost forty years later, I've been in full-time ministry for more than thirty-four years. Truth be told, I miss that young, naïve, Jesus-can-do-anything kid who followed the whisper of God about what brought him joy and wanted to change the world for Jesus. More often than I care to admit, I've been lulled into a religious vocation and drawn into institutional preservation. At nineteen, I believed "Jesus is Lord" down to my toes. My life was a mess. I was a dry drunk trying to manage my obsessions for alcohol, drugs, and sex with a white-knuckled grip on God. I often was lured into all three deadly obsessions, but I also had a relentless desire to see people know Jesus. In those days, no matter where I went, I talked about Jesus and the changes he was making in my life. Today, the "fire in my belly" more days than I care to admit has turned into a cozy, lukewarm fire.

What I love about fresh expressions is that it harnesses the primal impulses of faith in Jesus when it was a new adventure. Fresh expressions are messy. Pioneers are messy too. They color outside the lines. They monkey with established policies, naively chasing after God in places like flea markets, boat marinas, community gardens, and sports bars because they not only believe that "Jesus is Lord" but they behave like it too.

Missional Field Kit: Forming Your FX Team

The first step in engaging the new fields of a network society is simply gathering together a small group of fellow subversives who will join you in the cultivation of fresh expressions. At Wildwood, we had a handful of people serving on the Evangelism Committee who told me, "We're the ones who couldn't get on any of the good committees." Obviously, that's not a very positive perspective! We turned our Evangelism Committee into our Fresh Expressions team, which is now one of the most thriving groups in our church. Later, I'll suggest we need to think of this team as the "disruptive innovation" department of our church.

While it may not start in this way, we suggest your team grow to include people in each of these three spheres:

1. **Core:** solid followers of Jesus, may already be part of your church.
2. **Fringe of the Core:** these are people either new to the life of the church, or maybe not in your church. These folks have relationships in the community and know the landscape of practices there.

17

3. **Fringe:** these are people outside the life of your church who will be your "persons of peace" (Luke 10:1-12). They may not be Christian, but they open the door to the potential relational networks in your community.

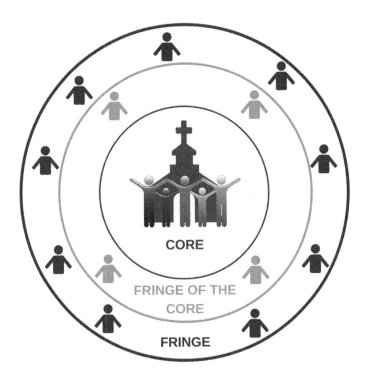

Further, you should also recruit onto the team persons who fulfill these three essential roles, which we will discuss in detail later:

1. **Pioneers:** people who are passionate about mission on the edges
2. **Supporters:** people who are passionate about supporting and releasing pioneers
3. **Permission Givers:** people who use their role to foster release of pioneers and to influence the system to be more willing to experiment

Your team could start by reading Luke 10:1-12 together. This is Jesus's missional blueprint for a pre-Christian world, but it also works for a post-Christian world! Study it. Reflect upon it. Digest it. It will undergird all further work your team will do together. Encourage each person on the team to read through this book and explore the missional field kit exercises together.[26]

---

26. For more Bible study suggestions, see Audrey Warren and Kenneth H. Carter, *Fresh Expressions: A New Kind of Methodist Church for People Called Methodists* (Nashville: Abingdon Press, 2018).

The Work of the Holy Spirit in the Space of Flows

The early Methodist movement included leaders who emphasized the person and work of the Holy Spirit. There are accounts of supernatural occurrences, including speaking in tongues, healings, exorcisms, prophecies, dreams, and miraculous escapes.[1] The whole movement was enabled by the Spirit. Lay preachers, some illiterate, were boldly proclaiming the gospel and ordinary folks did extraordinary things, accompanied by sweeping waves of conversions. Chilcote writes, "The Wesleys equated the Holy Spirit—third person of the Trinity—with God's empowering presence."[2]

Paul told the Corinthians that no one can say "Jesus is Lord" except by the Holy Spirit (1 Cor 12:3). The Spirit is the life force that flows through the body of Christ. Furthermore, renewal movements do not sweep the face of the earth by the sheer will power of human beings. Fortunately, we have a "helper" (John 14:16; 16:7) who "guides" us into "all truth" (John 16:13).

The Holy Spirit, this third person of the Trinity, is affirmed in the Nicene-Constantinopolitan Creed as the one who "proceeds from the

---

1. Daniel Jennings, *The Supernatural Occurrences of John Wesley* (CreateSpace, 2005).

2. Paul W. Chilcote, *Recapturing the Wesleys' Vision: An Introduction to the Faith of John and Charles Wesley* (Woodstock, VT: Skylight Paths Publishing, 2011), 92.

Father and the Son; who with the Father and the Son together is worshiped and glorified."[3] If we follow the sequence of Jesus's incarnation, death, resurrection, ascension, and sending of the Holy Spirit at Pentecost, we realize the Spirit (one with Jesus and yet distinct) makes the presence of Jesus available now. The risen Jesus is not confined to one place, in one moment in time, but has been downloaded into every living thing and permeates the entire cosmos (Eph 1:23). The experience of Jesus's resurrected presence sustained the early church and enabled their confession of his Lordship (1 Cor 12:3).

More precisely, the Holy Spirit is involved in the transformation of the entire cosmos and all living things (Rom 8:22-23). The Spirit is working, healing, and guiding all the universe to a final form of emergence—the new creation (Rev 22). This understanding of the Spirit informs a Wesleyan experience of prevenient grace.

Historically, Methodists conceptualize the work of the Holy Spirit in the realms of personal faith, the community of believers, and responsible living in the world.[4] Before we are even aware, through prevenient grace, the Holy Spirit is initiating a relationship with us. The Spirit makes life in Jesus possible. The Spirit woos us, compels us to embrace God's free offer of salvation in Christ, and then comes to indwell us in an intensely personal way through justifying grace (Rom 8:16).[5] The Spirit awakens our hearts to the love of God (Rom 5:5), thus beginning the transformative process of renewal from a current fallen nature into the image of Christ (Rom 8:29). This transformation is not an *event* but a *process.* God is working *within* us to accomplish a total restoration resulting in new creation, through sanctifying grace.[6]

---

3. Quoted in Ted Campbell, *Methodist Doctrine: The Essentials* (Nashville: Abingdon Press, 2011), 44.

4. *The Social Principles* (*The Book of Discipline, 2012*, ¶160–66, pp. 103–42).

5. "Witness of the Spirit, Discourse 1" (John Wesley and Kenneth C. Kinghorn, *The Standard Sermons in Modern English* [Nashville: Abingdon Press, 2002], 169).

6. T. Runyon, *The New Creation: John Wesley's Theology Today* (Nashville: Abingdon Press, 1998), 8.

As a practitioner of fresh expressions, I often have a front-row seat in watching people journey through these waves of grace—prevenient, justifying, and sanctifying—right before my eyes.

God the Spirit, the "wild child" of the Trinity, is always "going native." "Yet we hear them speaking in our own *native* languages!" (Acts 2:8 NLT, emphasis mine). The "subversive one" is a missionary spirit, operating outside the bounds, moving on the missional edge, bringing forth community among division, and enabling humanity to share the very *agape* of Christ.[7] In often prevenient ways, the Spirit is forming one authentic, diverse, peaceable community from all the peoples of the earth. The Holy Spirit is infilling and supernaturally enabling humanity to fulfill God's mission for the redemption of the world. Yet, the Holy Spirit manifests the Kingdom in "native" and "personal" ways. The Holy Spirit is never forcing some cultural perspective on another group of people but emerging out of who and what they already are. It is not the work of the Holy Spirit when missional leaders advance a colonial, attractional, propositional form of Christendom instead of incarnational living.[8]

Elaine Heath reminds us that at times the church has colluded with secular and military power, and "mission and evangelism" have been "hijacked to serve the interests of empire."[9] We have sometimes read the Great Commission in this way. This is an inaccurate depiction of our Christian faith that more resembles a Western narrative of power—a false narrative that deceives us into thinking the answer to most problems is the appropriate application of corporate power. If we use our power to do this, we can overcome that, solve this problem, fix that broken thing, and so on. If

7. Loida I. Otero, Z. Maldonado Pérez, et al., *Latina Evangélicas: A Theological Survey from the Margins* (Eugene, OR: Cascade, 2013), 28–32.

8. David J. Bosch, *Transforming Mission: Paradigm Shifts in Theology of Mission* (Maryknoll, NY: Orbis, 1991), 1.

9. Elaine A. Heath and Larry Duggins, *Missional, Monastic, Mainline: A Guide to Starting Missional Micro-Communities in Historically Mainline Traditions* (Eugene, OR: Cascade, 2014), 12.

we just use our power appropriately, we can "take back our community" for Jesus.

As Wesleyans, we believe the ultimate outworking of the Spirit's power is love. This love is a different kind of power—relational power—faithful presence—*withness*. It's also a love that goes first (1 John 4:9). God's love is already at work on the scene before we get there. We can't "take back the community for Jesus" because by the power of the Spirit the community already belongs to Jesus.

The Spirit always goes ahead of us and is already intimately involved in the life of every person we encounter. John Wesley became aware of this in a field outside Bristol. He found the Spirit at work in the lives of people beyond the church walls, inviting him to join what God was already up to. The Spirit was inviting him to "go native."

Because the world truly was his parish, Wesley's pulpit took many forms. His example is relevant to the new missional frontier in a network society. Because Wesley believed the Spirit went before him, many places became his *pulpit*. As Arthur Wood writes, "His real pulpit was where the people were."[10]

We use the "fields" as the metaphor for open air preaching, but this included many types of "pulpits." Here's a non-exhaustive list of places Wesley preached: parks, public and private gardens, churchyards, lofts, barrack-yards, barns, streets, theaters, private homes, front porches, city malls, general recreation grounds, miners' camps, prisons, paved stairs, gateways, mansions, open squares, guildhalls, marketplaces, covered shambles, piazzas, bridges, cottages, malt houses, castles, cemetery tomb-stones, market houses, universities, shooting ranges, libraries, schools, courthouses, session houses, exchanges, local assembly rooms, playhouses, ballrooms, workhouses, asylums, hospitals, and auditoriums. Also, he preached from many natural formations: rocks, hills, mountainsides, granite boulders, beaches, prehistoric mounds, stone hollows, riverbanks,

---

10. Arthur S. Wood, *The Burning Heart: John Wesley, Evangelist* (Minneapolis: Bethany Fellowship, 1978), 136.

fields, orchards, meadows, and the shade of convenient trees. Wesley did of course preach in Anglican parish churches, when they were open to him, but also, we find him in Presbyterian, Independent, Calvinist, Baptist, and Quaker meeting houses. Further, he preached in the Methodist buildings, sometimes when they were still under construction![11]

In the emerging Industrial Revolution of the eighteenth century, Wesley was leveraging the power of first, second, and third places. Not only did he understand the importance of embodying the gospel in the places where people lived, he also had the contextual intelligence to adapt to the rhythms of their lives. Wesley adjusted his schedule to times when he could reach the people. He preached every day—morning, noon, and night—wherever his voice could be heard by a crowd. He also habitually preached at 5:00 a.m., so he could catch the workers as they went off to work in the mines, forges, farms, and mills. This was so important to Wesley that he called the early morning gatherings "the glory of the Methodists" and said if this was ever abandoned, "Ichabod" (the glory of God has departed) should be inscribed over Methodist societies.[12]

On one occasion, Wesley discovered the early morning gathering had been abandoned at Stroud. He wrote, "Give up this, and Methodism too will degenerate into a mere sect, only distinguished by some opinions and modes of worship."[13] This foreshadows his more well-known and often quoted statement,

> I am not afraid that the people called Methodists should ever cease to exist either in Europe or America. But I am afraid lest they should only exist as a dead sect, having the form of religion without the power. And this undoubtedly will be the case unless they hold fast both the doctrine, spirit, and discipline with which they first set out.

This is an apt description of many churches today. A church without the Spirit is one "having the form of religion without the power." How did

---

11. Wood, *The Burning Heart*, 125–36.

12. Wood, *The Burning Heart*, 154.

13. Wesley, quoted in Wood, *The Burning Heart*, 154.

we "degenerate" into a Sunday morning attractional-only mode from this? Can we adapt some of these early practices for today?

The Holy Spirit is up to something out in the fields again, stirring up a movement out in the ordinary places where people do life.

Time for a Remix

So how do we "go native" in the power of the Spirit on the new missional frontier of a post-everything society? The Fresh Expressions movement resembles early Methodism's deep reliance on the person and work of the Holy Spirit.

God the Spirit is a pioneer. *The pioneer Spirit is calling us to the fields.*

The "fields" have changed. The massive social shifts have literally transformed the human experience of space and time. In a network society, we must now recognize the difference between two kinds of space: the *space of place* and the *space of flows.*

Castells believes that space, throughout human history, has been "the material support of simultaneity in social practice." So cities, for instance, are communication systems, increasing the chance of communication through physical contiguity (direct contact). He calls the *space of place* the space of contiguity.[14] Through the amalgamation of technologies listed earlier, along with computerized transportation, "simultaneity was introduced in social relationships at a distance" (distanced contact). Meaning, humans no longer need to interact face-to-face in a physical place to have "contact." This transformation of the spatiality of social interaction through simultaneity creates a new kind of space: *the space of flows.* Castells defines the space of flows as "the material support of simultaneous social practices communicated at a distance."[15]

---

14. Manuel Castells, *The Rise of the Network Society* (Oxford and Malden, MA: Blackwell, 2000), xxxi.

15. Castells, *The Rise of the Network Society,* xxxi.

Castells writes, "The key innovation and decision-making processes take place in face-to-face contacts, and they still require a shared space of places, well-connected through its articulation to the space of flows."[16] Microelectronic and communication technologies serve as *flows* that enable us to connect across geographies and time. Flows of capital, information, organizational interaction, images, sounds, and symbols move along a complex web of interconnected networks enabled by these technologies. Flows are the means through which the movement of people, objects, and things is accomplished from one node to another in social space. The network society is an interconnected matrix, activated by these technologically enabled flows. The flows are the social organization, the expression of processes dominating our economic, political, and symbolic life.[17]

Sociologist Ray Oldenburg furthers our understanding of the "space of place" in his description of first, second, and third places connected by flows of technology in a mobile culture. First Place is the home or primary place of residence. Second Place is the workplace or school place. Third Place may be public places separate from the two usual social environments of home and workplace which "host regular, voluntary, informal, and happily anticipated gatherings of individuals." Examples are environments such as cafes, pubs, theaters, parks, and so on.[18]

These "places" are the "fields" for us today, the "nodes" of a network society. These places are outside the earshot of church bells, where people gather for community. We need soft eyes to notice these Holy Spirit "hot spots," and access the kingdom WiFi there. In a mobile, hyperconnected, and diverse culture, a neighborhood approach to mission alone will not suffice. We still need an effective missional approach for the neighborhood focused on a specific people in a stationary place. We need also to cultivate a healthy missional approach for the network that allows us to adapt to

16. Castells, *The Rise of the Network Society*, xxxvi.

17. Castells, *The Rise of the Network Society*, 442.

18. Ray Oldenburg, *The Great Good Place: Cafés, Coffee Shops, Bookstores, Bars, Hair Salons, and Other Hangouts at the Heart of a Community* (New York: Marlowe, 1999), 16.

the emergent societal structure. This approach unleashes an exploration of endless new avenues for mission, a kaleidoscope of contextual variations for fresh expressions of church which come in all colors, shapes, and sizes.

The pioneer Spirit goes ahead of us in the space of flows in a network society. Knocking on the doors in the church neighborhood is in many contexts the least effective method to engage people. In the 5G speed of mobile culture, we are experiencing the largest urbanization trend in human history. Overpopulation of cities is leading to the creation of smaller dormitory-like home places, and how people dwell in these living quarters is changing.

Are we really present in our home places when we are physically there? For instance, if I'm in my home in Wildwood, Florida, but using Face-Time with my friend in London, what time zone am I in? Or if I'm corresponding through email with a friend in California, am I fully present in Florida? If I'm watching a livestream video of my colleague in Momostenango, Guatemala, leading a prayer march as it unfolds in real time, where is my consciousness? My body could be present as well, since I can literally fly in an airplane, jumping space and time, to any of these places in less than a day. Castells suggests that "computers, communications systems, and genetic decoding and programming are all amplifiers and extensions of the human mind."[19]

These technologies literally enable us to be present to some degree across the world at any given moment. A part of us, our technologically extended mind, is actually in both places simultaneously. The technology enables a kind of extension of ourselves to be present on the digital frontier. This leads to the compression and transformation of time, that is, "the development of flex-time, and the end of separation of working time, personal time, and family time, as in the penetration of all time/spaces by wireless communication devices that blur different practices in a simultaneous time frame through the massive habit of multi-tasking."[20]

---

19. Castells, *The Rise of the Network Society*, 31.

20. Castells, *The Rise of the Network Society*, xli.

Moynagh and Worsley describe a space in the network society as "a world above the world."[21] In the space of flows, Castells speaks of a "time-less time" and a distinction between the "instant time of computerized networks versus clock time of everyday life."[22]

These transformations can have a significantly adverse effect: a disem-bodied life. Thus, the very nature of a hyper-connected global community creates disjuncture by the loss of commitment to a particular locality. The separation caused by the emerging societal structure leads to *deterritorial-ization,* which refers to the disconnection between peoples, culture, and place. It means the distancing from one's locality made possible by these flows in virtual, cultural, and physical globalization.[23] If emerging genera-tions are spending ten hours per day on screens, how present are we to the physical environment and people where our bodies are at any given moment?[24]

In a culture where most people don't know their next-door neigh-bors *physically*, they have vast networks of next-door global neighbors *digitally*. Relationships are largely enabled and sustained through flows of communication technology. People connect physically through the flows, across geographies, to engage communal practices in neutral places. These network-based relationships bring healing to our isolation and sat-isfy our longing for human connection. If we believe the Spirit is at work in the seemingly random encounters of our day-to-day lives, why would we doubt that the Spirit is "going native" through these technologically enabled flows in the digital frontier? Why would we assume the Spirit is not present in the endless variety of contextual practices that relationships

21. Michael Moynagh and Richard Worsley, *Going Global: Key Questions for the Twenty-First Century* (London, UK: A & C Black, 2008), 3.

22. Castells, *The Rise of the Network Society,* 506.

23. Ryan K. Bolger, "Practice Movements in Global Information Culture: Looking Back to McGavran and Finding a Way Forward," *Missiology* 35, no. 2: 181–93 (2007), 188.

24. See https://www.cnn.com/2016/06/30/health/americans-screen-time-nielsen/index.html.

form around, such as yoga, dinner parties, soccer fields, coffee shops, and so on?

A networked missional approach is not a fresh concept, as we will see later through the missional approaches of Paul the Apostle and John Wesley. Yet it must begin where all mission should—with authentic relationship, desire to connect with and know and love our others. Any missional strategy that does not begin with an agenda-free love for others is questionable. We need simply to gather with a group of people and engage in the *practice* together, connected by *flows*, in the *places* where they do life.

A primary example of this practices is described in Luke 10:1-9, the missional blueprint of Jesus. The disciples, going out two-by-two, are instructed to locate a person "who shares God's peace" (Luke 10:6). For the first disciples, this was someone who opened his or her home, welcomed them at the table, and unlocked the relational potential of a community. In the network society, a peace-loving person can also open a network, a community of practice, teach us the language, and show us how things work around here. It is an utterly incarnational approach. We come empty handed as a learner into the world of the other (Luke 10:1-8). We take on a posture of vulnerability, with a single focus on forming a relationship. The Spirit works through that honest desire. If the Trinity is a revelation about God, God's way is a divine dance of loving relational power. The Spirit works through relationship, ushering in the kingdom in new, powerful ways as we reach out lovingly toward one other.

Wesley not only found ways to embody the church where the people were in his "world as parish" (the first, second, and third places of his day). He also adapted to the rhythms of their lives in the dawning of the Industrial Age (in his case, the 5:00 a.m. pre-work gatherings, "the glory of the Methodists"). In the Information Age, people move through the digital flows, in a 24/7 work culture at blazing 5G speed. Pioneers utilize these technologies to create a presence on the digital frontier. Using Instagram, Twitter, MeetUp, and Facebook events, they are planting new forms of church. Forming or incarnating themselves in micro-communities around shared interests, hobbies, and practices, "nones and dones" are forming relationships with Jesus through these pioneers (perhaps the equivalent of Wesley's lay preachers). This is unleashing once again the whole people of God, a movement among the "common people" in the fields.

Thus, through relationships with real people in the "nodes" (physical places) we spread the Christian faith like a good virus in the entry points that spreads through the "flows" (digital channels of connectivity) and heals the entire global network from the inside out.

Prayerfully seek what and where the Spirit is leading you. Ask what the Spirit is up to in the places where people do life. What are the rhythms of people's lives in our contexts? How are we engaging the neighborhoods of our communities? Also, how are we engaging the complex system of networks? In what ways are we utilizing the flows that connect people across geographies? What are practices in the zip codes within our reach, and how is the Spirit working through these practices to bring people together in relationship? How do we "go native" to join in the fun? Who are the "peace-makers"? Who are the "pioneers" for whom these practices are native?

Field Story—Beck

Imagine you are invited to one of our churches. Perhaps a friend invited you. Or perhaps you received a strange Facebook invite to this peculiar event. Perhaps you were just hungry for an amazing burrito. Nevertheless, you find yourself at Moe's Southwest Grill in Lady Lake, Florida, on a Sunday at 6:30 p.m. You're at church!

No usher meets you at the door, but the staff hollers out, "Welcome to Moe's!" There's no attendance pad to sign, but all of us check in on our social media accounts with one word about how we feel about being here today. There's no professional minister who stands up and tells us what the Bible means, but we read a couple verses of scripture from our screens and engage in a sermonic conversation. There's no altar with the signature Hawaiian bread and Welch's grape juice, but we have a full open table communion with the tortilla and Hi-C from the drink machine in the chalice. Many people have accepted Christ and taken communion right here. Sure, we don't have an offering plate, but we dump out the chips and salsa basket and pass the plate at the conclusion of our gathering.

It looks different, but this congregation meeting for the past seven years at Moe's is fully church in every way. It's called Burritos and Bibles.

This fresh expression started with a relationship. Dren was once the manager at Moe's. Jill (my wife and copastor) and I love burritos and all-you-can-eat chips and salsa. Sharing this meal is one of the "practices," and Moe's is one of our favorite "third places." Where else can you have the Lord's Supper while the music of Jimmy Hendrix, Michael Jackson, or Lynyrd Skynyrd plays in the background?

Every week, I went to Moe's during Dren's evening shift. We both embrace Star Wars. I happen to be a Sith Lord, and Dren is on the dark side as well. We would talk about our favorite past episodes and speculate about upcoming episodes. Occasionally, we digressed into conversations about Marvel Comics and that film dynasty. Over time, Dren and I built up a pretty cool relationship. He was a peace-loving person to me, and I was a peace-sharing person to him.

Everything changed the day Dren came to cater a lunch for clergy at our church facility. We had talked about the possibility. He personally committed to come himself, and he even offered to give us a significant budget break on our food. Dren walked into the fellowship hall and said, "Dude, you're the pastor here?" "Yep," I grinned. "That's pretty sketchy," he smirked. Dren is one of those people who always says what's on his mind. I suppose he's right, being a clergy person in the 2000s is suspicious.

Nevertheless, this initiated a conversation about faith and opened the door to the possibility of what would become Burritos and Bibles. Dren and I talked out what it could look like. He asked good questions. We set good boundaries. This would be a mutually beneficial relationship. We would meet in a slow time for the restaurant and try to fill it with new people. He would work out a discount on our food. We would not engage people in the space unless they engaged us. We would not be disruptive. We would pray for Dren, the employees, the business, and the chain. Dren ran this idea up the corporate ladder and got the green light!

Dren was not really a Christian when we started. Like most young people today, he didn't go to church; he worked two jobs, seven days a week! At about a year into our weekly gatherings, Dren's grandfather got sick. He approached our group, and said, "Hey I know you guys do the prayer thing. Would you pray for my grandfather?" We did pray. A lot. And over time, Dren started to take communion with us. He suggested that his co-workers could take communion with us. "Guys, I just did the communion thing; you can go try it if you want to." Yes, a captive audience for communion! We have discovered that most people find an invitation to a Sunday morning service "sketchy." However, they are much more open to conversations about Jesus around tables laden with burritos and all-you-can-eat chips and salsa. They will even invite their friends.

Because of Dren, our "peace-maker," and the micro-culture built up around the practice of eating amazing Tex-Mex, many people came to know Jesus over seven years. People who don't go to church have found a church. People discovered again that God loves them. People prayed for the first time. People learned the scriptures. They also discovered Christians really aren't that bad, after all. Some found their way to the "mother ship" (I prefer Death Star) we call Wildwood United Methodist Church.

Looking back, I can see how the Spirit was at work. The Spirit was at work in Dren as we built a relationship. The Spirit was at work in the people who just happened to wander into a space where church was happening. Some of those people accepted Jesus, took communion with us, or found a new group of friends. Some heard the Lord's Prayer again for the first time in years. The Spirit was working through the employees who found a church home in the restaurant where they work. The Spirit was at work when after a year of meeting, someone said, "Hey, this is our church, right? Shouldn't we take up an offering or something?" We then dumped out the chips and salsa basket and passed the collection plate.

The Spirit was at work through the flows, the web of interconnected technologies that connected us here: the tweets, the texts, the Facebook event invites, and the page "check ins." The Spirit was at work in the nudges along the way: "Let's try prayer next week"..."Can we read a couple verses from the Bible tonight?"..."Next week we are going to try this thing called the Lord's Supper"...and so on.

Thanks for coming to our church, hope you stop by again sometime soon!

Missiography—Releasing the APEs (Acevedo)

The Holy Spirit gifts the church to become fully mature. Paul brilliantly describes how the church, the Body and Bride of Christ, functions in Ephesians 4. The goal of the church is to produce fully cruciformed followers of Jesus. Buildings, programs, budgets, staff, and more serve this chief Kingdom end. Paul describes five offices or roles Jesus gives to believers:

> He gave some apostles, some prophets, some evangelists, and some pastors and teachers. His purpose was to equip God's people for the work of serving and building up the body of Christ until we all reach the unity of faith and knowledge of God's Son. God's goal is for us to become mature adults—to be fully grown, measured by the standard of the fullness of Christ. (Eph 4:11-13)

Apostles, prophets, evangelists, pastors, and teachers are the Spirit-gifted followers of Jesus that make up the body of Christ. By using Al Hirsch's acrostic, these service roles taken together can be shortened and called APEST. These offices or roles cooperate together synergistically to make mature apprentices of Jesus.

I spend a lot of my time with remarkable leaders in local churches, and, to a person, the greatest concern I hear over and over again is about the difficulty churches have in helping people grow to maturity or what Paul "measured by the standard of the fullness of Christ." Even with the tools and training shared by amazing churches and conferences, honest church leaders consistently bemoan their struggle to help grow mature disciples of Jesus.

Could it be that the offices or roles described by Paul in Ephesians are not being released? Some say our churches have been led primarily by the shepherds and teachers, but the apostles, prophets, and evangelists (the APEs) have either been domesticated or run off.

I'm a shepherd and teacher to the core. Everything from my training and mentors shaped and formed me for this kind of ministry. I like order and results. I like my office and my church—a lot! APEs on the other hand are entrepreneurial. They go with the flow. They thrive in chaos. They harness charisma, which is always unstable. They want to take on hell and the devil with a squirt gun. They mess with my deep need for order and, if I'm honest, control. They like being out in the community and hanging out with messy people who seem really far from God.

So I am asking the Holy Spirit to allow me to cultivate an intentional environment at Grace Church that releases the APEs instead of domesticating or running them off. We tend to attract people to us who are like us, so it takes intentionality to discover, develop, and deploy people who are not like ourselves. For me, these are the APEs. This means being more comfortable with chaos. It means being patient about results. It means practicing active listening skills as I get to know the heart and mind of the APEs in our midst.

Here's where this connects with fresh expressions of church. I have to wonder: how many APEs are sitting in the pews of our churches waiting to be released? Release the APEs!

Missional Field Kit
Finding Holy Spirit Hot Spots

Instructions: You need a large white board, or stick-up paper, and markers. Gather your team, pray, and read Luke 10:1-12 together. Ask for someone to volunteer as the resident artist. Where are the "fields" (first, second, and third places) that you have access to? These are the "hot spots" of the Holy Spirit. In a network society connected by flows, we are always looking for WiFi to "connect." Pray together, try to discern where you can connect and download what the Spirit is up to....

1. Draw your home base.

2. Draw out potential first, second, and third places where people gather.

3. Is there any place on the map where someone on the team goes frequently?

4. Do you have a "peace-making person" in one of these locations already?

5. Prayerfully decide which possibilities have the most potential.

6. Who will take responsibility for the potential locations, networks, and people?

7. What's the next logical step?

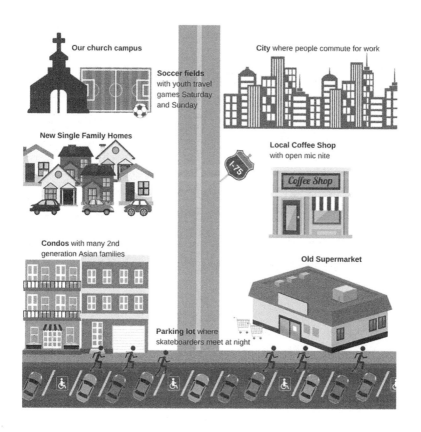

DOWNLOAD 3

A God-Shaped Church— One and Threeness

Our beliefs about God should shape how we live in the world. John Wesley experienced God as a seeking and sending God, whose essential nature is love. That mindset fueled his actions. Critics of Wesley's field preaching argued that there was enough room for everyone in the parish system, and all had equal opportunity to come. Their primary understanding was attractional: build the sanctuaries and they would or should come. In defense of field preaching, Wesley wrote,

> Will you say (as I have known some tender-hearted Christians), "Then it is their own fault; let them die, and be damned"? I grant that it is their own fault; and so was it my fault and yours when we went astray like sheep that were lost. Yet the Shepherd of souls sought after us, and went after us in the wilderness. And "oughtest not thou to have compassion on thy fellow servants, as he had pity on thee?" Ought we not also "to seek," as far as in us lies, "and to save that which is lost"?[1]

The Wesleyan understanding of the triune God is not revolutionary. It is remarkable because it emerged from how John Wesley weaved together the Eastern Fathers, Pietists, Puritans, Caroline Divines, Cambridge

---

1. John Wesley, *Works*, Vol. VIII, p. 113, *A Farther Appeal to Men of Reason and Religion* (1745).

Platonists, and the various streams of high church Anglicanism, blending them into a "practical divinity." Charles Wesley weaved this distinct mixture of practical theology throughout the massive collection of hymns he wrote. The people called Methodists primarily preserved their brand of practiced faith by singing it from one generation to the next through their rich hymnody. This enabled uneducated and even illiterate persons to access the core marks and habits of early Methodism.

Methodists continue to emphasize a personal experience of a *seeking* and *sending* trinitarian God, whose primary characteristic is relentless *love*. We experience the missional love of God through "waves of grace" (prevenient, justifying, and sanctifying) and "means of grace" (prayer, searching scripture, communion, fasting, and holy conversation). The discipleship process is connected to these means of grace and waves of grace—the profuse outflow of God's unconditional love.

Will Willimon discusses the "processional" or "sent" work of the Trinity, emphasizing the Wesleyan heritage of a "sent" rather than "called" ministry. Being on the move, itinerating from place to place was born from Wesley's dynamic seeking and sending trinitarianism.[2] The Trinity as missionary seeks *and* sends the church. At the conclusion of every worship experience at Wildwood, we observe Holy Communion. We remember at the table how God sought us, put on flesh to get to us, and how Jesus heals the breach in our relationship. Then we turn and face the door as reconciled people for the benediction, the sending forth. I always reiterate that just outside that door is the third largest mission field in the world. Many Americans don't know God lovingly put on flesh in refusal to be separated from them and is available to transform their lives. Thus, every Sunday we remember together that our relational and missionary God has invited us to join this mission (Matt 28:18-20). As God the creator's "sent" people,

---

2. William H. Willimon, *United Methodist Beliefs: A Brief Introduction* (Louisville, KY: Westminster John Knox, 2007), 6.

we as the body of Christ, go out, guided and infilled by the Holy Spirit (John 20:21b-22).[3]

Wesley believed with all Christians in one true and living God, infinite in power, wisdom, goodness, and love—God is the creator and sustainer of all things. This relational triune God's oneness is expressed in three Persons, of one substance, power, and eternity.[4] Exodus 3:1-15 describes God's seeking of an orphaned Egyptian fugitive named Moses to send on an impossible mission. God hears the cry of the people, God seeks, and God sends. This portrait of an astonishingly compassionate God who is vulnerable to the pain of people, using a misfit as a chosen instrument, deeply resonates with my own experience of God. I, too, in the presence of an awesomely holy God was relentlessly sought and sent. I, too, cried "Why me? Who am I?" and received the same simple answer, "Because I'll be with you" (Exod 3:12).

I preached a sermon on this passage in the first-person narrative titled "The Worst Man for the Perfect Job." In that sermon, as Moses, I was carrying on a deep conversation about the brokenness of my distant past with the sheep I was herding. Suddenly, God appeared in the burning bush! In my exchange with God, I wrestled with God's self-identification as "I am that I am." While there is no space here to explicate the variety of interpretations of this name-formula, "this enigmatic name demonstrates power, fidelity, and presence."[5] Also it is a crucial focal point for the un-folding self-revelation of God's intervening action in history articulated in the scriptures.

God is in an interconnected matrix of relationship we call the Trinity. We seek to understand this relationality within the Godhead as the *peri-choresis*—the circle dance of the trinitarian life. *Perichoresis* refers to the

---

3. *United Methodist Hymnal*, "Word and Table II," 14: "That we may be for the world the body of Christ."

4. *The Book of Discipline, 2012*, ¶103.

5. *Exodus. New Interpreters Commentary: General Articles and Introduction, Commentary, and Reflections for Each Book of the Bible, Including the Apocryphal/Deuterocanonical Books* (Nashville: Abingdon Press, 1994), 714.

"mutual interpenetration" or the way the three Persons of the Trinity relate to one another. This is an image of God as "community of being" in which each Person although one, remains distinct, penetrates and is penetrated by the other.[6] It is a blending of diversity and oneness. In God's *I Am*-ness, we discover a community of diverse singularity—the three-yet-one.

The ministry of Wesley, both in the cathedrals of the established church, and out in the fields, reawakened an understanding of this three-in-one seeking and sending God, whose primary characteristic is active, initiating love. Most of the fellow ministers of Wesley's day were deeply locked into an "attractional only" form of church, waiting for not-yet-Christians to stumble into the ranks of their dwindling flocks. This approach misses the central essence of God's seeking and sending nature, and how the church is an extension of God's graceful activity in the earth.

There is another move in God's seeking and sending self-revelation: the outpouring of the Holy Spirit and the sending of the church. The church is quite literally another incarnation of Jesus, the Body of Christ in the world. This understanding of God influenced Wesley's view of the church as a "redeemed and redeeming fellowship." He held an "instrumental" view of the church.[7] The early Methodist movement enabled the church to embody both the seeking and sending nature of God—a God shaped church.

Time for a Remix

The Fresh Expressions movement allows the church to recover a robust understanding of the seeking and sending nature of the Trinity. Just as God's own life is a communion in which oneness and diversity are shared in a divine dance of "making room" for one another, so inherited congregations planting fresh expressions cultivate this kind of relational

6. Alister E. McGrath, *Christian Theology: An Introduction* (Malden, MA: Wiley-Blackwell, 2011), 241.

7. Paul Avis, *The Oxford Handbook of Ecclesiology* (Oxford: Oxford University Press, 2018), 322, 331.

interaction with their larger community. The perichoretic nature of the Trinity demonstrates how in God's own eternal being there is a movement of seeking and sending. Father sends the Son, Father and Son send the Spirit. The Spirit seeks and descends upon Jesus in the murky waters of his baptism (Luke 3:22). The father of the prodigal keeps his eyes on the road, watching for the son, and while he's still a far way off, he runs to him (Luke 15:20-21). There is a profound giving and receiving of love in which God "makes room."

The Risen Jesus breathes the Holy Spirit on the disciples and says, "As the Father sent me, so I am sending you" (John 20:21). Mission is linked with the Trinity, and this realization gives new life to the modern missional church movement. Mission is no longer subservient to ecclesiology or soteriology. Rather, mission is the purpose of church alignment and life together with Christ. David Bosch writes, "The classical doctrine on the *missio Dei* as God the Father sending the Son, and God the Father and the Son sending the Spirit was expanded to include yet another 'movement': Father, Son, and Holy Spirit sending the church into the world."[8] This understanding was embodied in the fields of the early Methodist movement. In some ways, it led to the restructuring of the church around the new organizing principle of mission, the outworking nature of God's seeking and sending love.

The recovering of this movemental understanding unleashed the Evangelical Revival in England. The stagnation of the church was stirred to movement again. The scattered groups of people in the fields, miners' camps, and town squares interacted synergistically with the gatherings of worshippers under their steeples. Over time, the movement was institutionalized, settling the activity in the fields for church sanctuaries. However, this attractional form of church can be separated from mission until it no longer resembles the movemental nature of God.

---

8. David J. Bosch, *Transforming Mission: Paradigm Shifts in Theology of Mission* (Maryknoll, NY: Orbis, 1991), 390.

The shape of the church today can be reflected in the relational dance of the Trinity. If we were to recover the form of the church, as derived from the very *perichoresis* of "interpenetration" and the "community of being," of Father, Son, and Spirit, would this be a God-shaped church?

Lincoln Harvey sees the "mixed economy" or what we call the "blended ecology" as reflecting God's very nature.[9] This "shape" of the church, with stationary and emerging modes dancing together, reflects the dynamic, movemental, and loving interrelationship that is the seeking and sending heart of the Trinity. The blended ecology is a demonstration of this flow of mutual giving between the inherited and emerging modes of the church. It creates a dynamic otherness which "makes room." One mode in isolation is a parody of God's nature. Both together, interacting in rhythms of space making, actually draw communities into the life of God. More simply, the shape of the church is derived from the Trinity as missionary—a shape that is both fixed and fluid, the blended ecology.[10]

The Holy Spirit dances between the fresh expressions and the inherited congregation, seeking and sending. The triune God, a life of shared love, not self-contained individuals, draws the community into that life. As Migliore writes, "just as the life of the triune persons is life with, for, and in each other, so the church is called to life in communion in which persons flourish in mutually supportive relationships with others. In such communion, the church becomes *imago Trinitatis,* an analogy of, and partial participation in, the triune life of God."[11]

Leslie Newbigin wrote, "The idea that one can or could at any time separate out by some process of distillation a pure gospel unadulterated by any cultural accretions is an illusion. It is, in fact, an abandonment of

9. Lincoln Harvey, "How Serious Is It Really? The Mixed Economy and the Light-Hearted Long Haul," in Graham Cray, Ian Mobsby, and Aaron Kennedy, *Fresh Expressions of Church and the Kingdom of God*, 95–105 (Norwich: Canterbury, 2012), 98.

10. Michael Beck, *Deep Roots, Wild Branches: Revitalizing the Church in the Blended Ecology* (Franklin, TN: Seedbed, 2019).

11. Referencing John Zizioulas, *Being as Communion: Studies in Personhood and the Church* (1985) in Daniel L. Migliore, *Faith Seeking Understanding: An Introduction to Christian Theology* (Grand Rapids, MI: Eerdmans, 2014), 274–75.

the gospel, for the gospel is about the word made flesh."[12] The church is in some sense always shaped by the age in which it's emerging afresh. As we will see more fully, the Methodist movement harnessed the energy of change as society moved into the Industrial Age. The "connection" of Methodist polity was a reflection of the larger industrial networks taking shape.

While the church's form has always grown out of its interaction with context, the danger is the corruption of the church by the context. As Hans Küng noted, cultural adaptation is not always good, "for that could mean adapting itself to the evil, the anti-God elements, the indifferentism in the world."[13]

Emerging generations describe the vast disconnect between the Jesus of scripture and the church of North America or Europe. Like it or not, the church lost its prophetic street cred and backbone. Even more damaging, in the search for political power we lost our legitimating narrative beneath many layers of corrupt imperial perversions.

Alan Roxburgh discusses at length how Protestant denominations in the United States adopted the organizational structure of the twentieth-century corporation and benefited greatly. By adopting this corporate structure, we helped churches to thrive in that season, as the legitimating narrative of United States capitalist culture became a seemingly perfect bedfellow for the church. Churches took up the language of rationalized efficiency, professional management, and bureaucratic structures.[14] The attractional, "build it and they will come" model worked well in a Christendom culture that emerged in American democracy. However, this societal form is passing into irrelevance as the network society emerges. The hub and spoke, hierarchical structure of the corporation is fading from view. The new shape of society is networked, dispersed, and polycentric.

---

12. Lesslie Newbigin, *Foolishness to the Greeks: The Gospel and Western Culture* (Grand Rapids, MI: Eerdmans, 1986), 4.

13. Hans Küng, *The Church* (Garden City, NY: Image Books, 1976), 12.

14. Alan J. Roxburgh, *Structured for Mission: Renewing the Culture of the Church* (Downers Grove, IL: InterVarsity, 2015), 79.

Once again, we must adapt to the societal shifts taking place all around us at the speed of digital optics. Yet, we need not abandon fixed for fluid, because we live in both worlds simultaneously. We need both forms of church. This both/and way—worshipping in a parish congregation and in the fields—is not only profoundly Methodist, it is the deepest narrative of scriptural teaching about the blended ecology.

In *Deep Roots, Wild Branches: Revitalizing the Church in the Blended Ecology,* I posited that in the Bible we find a community defined by Jerusalem *and* Antioch, the gathered *and* the scattered, the inherited *and* the missional, the attractional *and* the contextual. The blended ecology is a life-giving remix. It's gathered *and* scattered, it's inherited *and* missional, it's attractional *and* contextual.

In the Old Testament, on the way to the promised land, God dwells in a tent, a *tabernacle.* God and the community who bears God's name are *missional*—a mobile force moving from place to place on the desert frontier. God also takes up residence for a while in a *temple*—a stationary place, God's primary zip code, where all people would be drawn to worship. God is an *attractional* force in a particular locality, Mount Zion, until the Babylonian captivity, when the people are dispersed, and God's house is destroyed. Then we see the emergence of the *synagogue,* a word that describes both a place and a people. The *synagogue* combined a more localized, contextual space, and held the pilgrimage to the temple as an expectation. We see how this both/and arrangement functioned in Jesus's own life in each of the Gospels.

In the New Testament, there is a compelling portrait of the blended ecology evidenced by Jerusalem *and* Antioch. The first Jerusalem council offers us a model for how the blended ecology can work together in a synergistic way (Acts 15). Jerusalem, representing the inherited church, confers to decide what to do with a swell of Gentile converts in Antioch, the emerging church. Jerusalem, as the attractional center in continuity with Israel, decides to support, embrace, and guide what's happening in Antioch. Antioch decides to collaborate and be in relationship with the "institution," if you will. Antioch is a very different contextual form of church. It is an indigenous manifestation of the context, with very different ideas, different language, and different people. The two modes learn to live together, and the rest is history.

THE BLENDED ECOLOGY

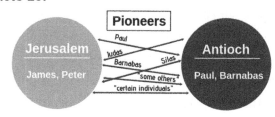

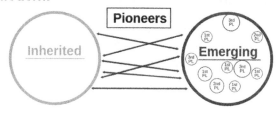

This image illustrates the interactions we see in Acts 15, and the modern form of pioneers moving between the two modes. We will explore this more fully in the next download.

Perhaps the most compelling image of this both/and way is centered in the incarnation of Jesus himself. Jesus's own life and ministry included synagogue and temple, coexisting together. Jesus worked in the fields of his day, while also teaching (and instigating holy mischief) in the temple. He embodied the church among the people, on mountain sides, lakes, front porches, and in the synagogues. Jesus, the most *attractive* human being that ever was *and* the manifestation of God's *missional* heart was the embodied fulfillment of temple, tabernacle, and Torah. His body itself was the new temple or tabernacle (Luke 22:19; John 2:19). Jesus was the stationary, mobile, enfleshed, incarnational, attractional, emerging flesh-and-blood tabernacle, temple, synagogue—fully human, fully God, one. Now the church is the continued embodiment of Jesus, "the body of Christ" (1 Cor 12:27) and "temple of the Holy Spirit" (1 Cor 6:19).

To be a *God-shaped church* is to be one and diverse, seeking and sending, mobile and stationary, attractional and emerging, fresh and vintage.

Re-engineering an entire congregation is easier said than done. Fortunately, we don't need to do this! We need to care for the center and stimulate the edge—which is again easier said than done. This is where a "fresh expressions" team can be solely dedicated to stimulating this missional activity. The activity of this team will eventually feed back into the congregation, transforming both.

The concept of disruptive innovation can illustrate this. Field preaching served as a form of disruptive innovation in Wesley's day. In our time, one need only briefly survey the landscape of the corporate world to catch a glimpse of the massive shifts occurring in the network society. Today, even the most agile organizations are outpaced by the technological forces revolutionizing the world around us in real time. One significant mistake can lead to a death-dealing scenario. Small entrants are able to take advantage of these shifts to harness emerging technologies to displace large, powerful, established incumbents.

Littering the North American business world are the tombstones of companies that were unable to stay on the edge of innovation. Companies that are frequently used as illustrations here are Blockbuster, Kodak, and Borders Group. In some sense these entities were transitional, meaning they utilized interim technologies. They are now just a few examples of once great organizations that epically failed to adapt or tried to hold on to early success. The interim technologies they utilized were simply replaced by forces of technological innovation, propped up by tax free laws or subsidies beyond their control.

Blockbuster passed on an opportunity to purchase Netflix; instead they were bankrupted by them. While Kodak actually developed the first interim version of digital cameras, companies like Canon rode the wave of the digital image revolution. The Borders Group of bookstores, Waldenbooks, Borders Express, and Borders airport and outlet stores, had opportunities to expand into the online market but fell off the innovational edge and were essentially steamrolled by Amazon. Some would add Christian denominations among the tombstones of has-beens.

In the *Harvard Business Review*, Clayton Christensen (et al.) clarifies some common misconceptions about disruptive innovation. Essentially, they define the phenomenon as a process where smaller emerging companies challenge established corporations by harnessing innovative technology. Established corporations tend to focus on their most profitable existing customers. Most of their energy, creativity, and effort are around improving their products or services for those existing customers. In that focus, incumbents place themselves outside the purchase capability of poorer, overlooked segments. Entrants then simply target those overlooked segments, which proves disruptive for the incumbent.[15]

For example, why go to Blockbuster and rent materials that I will most likely return for a late fee, when I can have all those rentable materials streamed into my home for one low monthly fee with Netflix? No searching the aisles, seeking to locate the prefect movie for my family only to find an empty box. No "be kind, rewind" campaign.

So, the entrant can focus on functionality of a product or service at a lower price. Larger corporations cannot typically respond efficaciously to the disruption, which goes mainstream by engaging a larger segment for a more reasonable price. In that scenario disruption has occurred.

By comparison, when John Wesley decided to "become more vile" and take up "field preaching," a disruptive innovation occurred. He began to reach a mass segment of the population that the larger church was

---

15. Clayton M. Christensen, Michael E. Raynor, and Rory McDonald, "What Is Disruptive Innovation?" *Harvard Business Review*, December 2015. Accessed October 20, 2017. https://hbr.org/2015/12/what-is-disruptive-innovation.

not reaching. The institutional fixation on buildings, education of clergy, and caring for the wealthy members of the church allowed the Methodist movement to thrive among the poor. While the larger church was targeting a smaller segment of already Christians, Wesley was targeting the masses of uneducated working-class people. With the "plain words" of the gospel, he went to the miners' camps, debtors' prisons, and street corners where the people lived. He got out in the flows. He then manifested the church in the neighborhoods and networks of the emerging industrial society, circumventing the bureaucracy of the attractional model.

It's not hard to see that much of the current institutional church is targeting a "high end market" of educated people with money, and more specifically catering to the needs of already Christians. While God loves this people group and they should certainly be a focus for the church, we are often missing the bigger picture. The Western churches' strategy is focused on a false assumption, that there are Christians out there who need a good church. The demographic of those who identify as Christian is decreasing every year, while the population grows massively. We are overshooting vast segments of the population, fighting for the little population of already Christians. That's why Fresh Expressions aims to reach the "nones and dones." Just as disruptive innovations originate in low-end or new markets, so the emerging missional movements are putting the church in the places where people do life together—livestreamed right into their relational living rooms, so to speak. The focus is not attracting Christians from other congregations, it's reaching new people who don't go to church.

Our advisers in the *Harvard Business Review* remind us, "'Disruption is a process.' The term 'disruptive innovation' is misleading when it is used to refer to a product or service at one fixed point, rather than to the evolution of that product or service over time."[16] We see that process actually unfold in the early Methodist revival. It's not about creating a product or giving birth to a new denomination; it's a process to reach overlooked segments of society.

---

16. Christensen, Raynor, and McDonald, "What Is Disruptive Innovation?"

Some of the largest, most successful corporations are getting ahead of disruptive innovation by creating departments that make disruptive innovation the focus of their experimentation and development. "Our current belief is that companies should create a separate division that operates under the protection of senior leadership to explore and exploit a new disruptive model."[17]

This business analogy compares to what a fresh expressions team can accomplish in a congregation. The inherited congregation provides the rooted depth and focuses primarily on care of existing members, while the emerging micro-communities serve as the research and development branch. We can have our corporate structure and a disruptive innovation department operating together in a symbiotic, life-giving way. Most if not all of our energies in the current paradigm are focused on caring for the members of a congregation. As a local clergy person, this can easily consume my whole week if I let it. However, many churches die in the process of being cared for by their pastor. We need to do both: care for the center and stimulate the edge.

John Wesley is an early example of this approach. While serving as an Anglican priest until the day he died, he experimented out in the fields with the disruptive innovation that became a future iteration of the established church.

We looked at the examples of Blockbuster, Kodak, and Borders Group, and how corporations like Netflix, Canon, and Amazon harnessed the disruptive innovation to flourish while the older established companies stuck to their business plans.

One of the massive implications of a disruptive innovation is that it allows the one harnessing its revolutionary force to gain access directly to the consumer. The disruptive innovation process typically harnesses a technology that circumvents the current structures and bureaucracies. When this occurs, it changes the market and the entire system has to respond to the innovation. Forward-looking, proactive organizations can

---

17. Christensen, Raynor, and McDonald, "What Is Disruptive Innovation?"

harness the energy, ride the shift, and capitalize on the new emerging scenario. Rigid institutions that misunderstand their own purpose and base their identity in how they have been successful in the previous market will ultimately fail.

This is where Jesus's forgotten beatitude is of the utmost importance: "Happy are the flexible, for they won't get bent out of shape." (I know Jesus said this somewhere, but nobody wrote it down.)

Unfortunately, the US church has not been very flexible or more precisely, not very responsive to the disruptive innovations all around us. We have lost the improvisational, responsive, highly adaptive model of the early Methodists, and fallen more into the institutional hierarchy that John Wesley challenged in his day.

Fresh Expressions is a form of disruptive innovation. It puts us directly in the living rooms, running groups, restaurants, fitness clubs, tattoo parlors, and social spheres where people are doing life together, connected by flows. Jesus loves the people of those communities, and he created the church as an instrument to reach them. We have something to offer humanity: a revolutionary force of love that can change their lives forever. It's something the church alone can give. We must rekindle the innovative nature of the primitive church to reach people in fresh ways.

Fresh expressions springing up in the first, second, and third places interact synergistically with the inherited church. Pioneer teams are sent out into the community as instruments of God's seeking love. The local church becomes an equipping and sending hub for these local missionaries. The life of the church spills into the community; the community spills into the church. "Church" is no longer confined to a compound where people gather for a regular rhythm, but Jesus communities are springing up everywhere throughout the larger communal ecosystem. Every place becomes a potential "burning bush" where the seeking "I Am" God of Moses is calling fugitives into a relationship.

This allows the church to reflect the *shape* of the Trinity. The church is the people God has sought and sent as "temple of the Holy Spirit" and "body of Christ" in the world. This enables a recovery of the "priesthood of all believers" that we will explore more fully next.

Here's a glimpse of what a blended ecology ecosystem in the network society can look like.

THE BLENDED ECOLOGY ECOSYSTEM

Field Story—Beck

It's easier to share the success stories, but we have failed more times than we've succeeded. In fact, on the new missional frontier, failure is not only an option, it is expected. We are invited to join this incredible seeking and sending activity of God, knowing in advance that we will make mistakes.

Our team had an idea for a fresh expression in which we would be an incarnate presence of God's love in the Wildwood homeless camps. We envisioned a church forming there in an organic way. We began to visit the camps and get to know some of the residents. Some were content with their nomadic lifestyle. One gentleman was not. He expressed a desire to get a job and just needed help. We secured a place and some necessities for him. Having no experience with church, he cautiously began to attend Wildwood. Soon he came to me and expressed his desire to receive Christ and be baptized; we then began that conversation.

Unfortunately, this relationship was perceived in the community experiencing homelessness as an "extraction" of one of their own from their community. We didn't listen well. Our focus was more about a "goal" to plant a fresh expression than to simply form relationships and be a witness. In our excitement to "Christianize" this man we brought harm to the community. We were no longer welcome.

The fresh expression idea failed, but a relationship was formed. By January, my new friend responded to the relentless, seeking love of God and was baptized. Weeks later, we led a team into the local jail, where his pregnant fiancé also accepted Christ. She was reborn into our community at Easter. God refused to give up on these two; God sought and recovered them.

This pattern is typical of fresh expressions of church: even when we "fail," even when we get it wrong, God can do incredible things with a simple desire to join the search and recovery efforts of Jesus. If our team had not had a bold vision to go and be church with people who would never come to church, would people like this couple, people beloved of God who may find themselves in a hard place, ever walk into our churches on a Sunday morning? The likelihood is very low. However, if we take seriously God's heart, and the seeking and sending nature of his relentless love, we cannot sit back and wait. It is our Wesleyan way to join God in the fields.

Learning is actually a process of failing forward. We have had many "failed" fresh expressions that resulted in connecting with folks like these two. We have learned to celebrate each stage of the journey: listening, loving, serving, and building relationships. Now we see these activities themselves as our "goals." Whether a fresh expression takes shape or not, these are things Jesus has called us to do. They are in fact an extension of Jesus's own search and recovery efforts.

These failures continually remind us of the seeking love of the good shepherd. Jesus teaches us that good shepherds risk leaving the ninety-nine to go after a lost one (Luke 15:4). If someone from the shepherd's board of professional responsibility heard Jesus's story that day, he or she would have been upset. "No good shepherd leaves the ninety-nine to go after a single lost sheep; that's shepherd malpractice!" It's foolish to risk the safety of the whole flock to go after a lone stray sheep. It doesn't make sense. It's not practical. Yet, Jesus, the good shepherd, does go after lost ones. He came after us, didn't he?

The liberating God who relentlessly sought us has sent us. At Wildwood, as we face the door for the benediction to go out in mission to the world together, we go with the God who goes to any length to find and reconcile one lost one.

Missiography—Attractional and Missional Church (Acevedo)

The church I serve has several "recovery communities." For nearly twenty years, we have aggressively sought to help people in need of recovery from addictions, afflictions, and compulsive behaviors to find a people, place, and process to heal. When I am honored to speak at one of these recovery communities, as is our tradition, I introduce myself by saying, "Hi. My name is Jorge and I'm a grateful follower of Jesus in recovery from drugs, alcohol, and codependency." The crowd always enthusiastically responds back with "Hi, Jorge."

When invited to speak at church conferences, I am often tempted to follow the tradition of our recovery communities and introduce myself in a similar but different way. It goes like this. "Hi. I'm Jorge and I am a grateful Christian pastor in recovery from an attractional-only ministry." Let me explain.

There is much discussion (sometimes controversy) about attractional church and missional church. In its most simple form, attractional church is a "come to us" strategy to reach people. Religious professionals like myself have been trained in seminaries and other educational environments to create sacred spaces for people to encounter God. Think of the temple that Solomon built in the Old Testament. It was a place and space for people to "come to" and experience God.

In my weekly rhythms as a church pastor, I spend five hours a week planning worship services with our teams and about ten to twelve hours a week planning and writing messages for these worship services. Our aim is to create a space and place for transcendent encounters with God the Father, Son, and Holy Spirit. After thirty-five years of doing this, I am still amazed that people actually show up for one of our four weekly worship gatherings. I am doubly amazed at how God uses these attractional, "come to us" experiences.

If attractional church is "come to us" church, then missional church is "come to you" church. It's moving church from the seats to the streets. Frankly, very little that I learned in either my undergraduate or graduate school ministry preparation taught me about missional ministry. I learned at school and on the job to prepare and execute sermons, administer the sacraments, lead committees, raise resources, and build a vital congregation. I was trained to "match, hatch, and dispatch" the people God.

Missional church happens in pubs, dog parks, community centers, pizza parlors, and flea markets. It releases apostles, prophets, and evangelists to establish new spaces for new people, many of whom are not likely to attend our "come to us" worship and discipleship experiences. When you think of missional church, think of the meeting tent or tabernacle that Moses established and moved about as the cloud of darkness by day and pillar of fire by night guided God's people through the wilderness. It was a portable, "on the move" worship space.

When I say that I am in recovery from an attractional-only ministry, I mean it. My default as a leader is still toward our "temple" ministry, yet

I am slowly learning and seeing the kingdom impact of our "tabernacle" ministry. I'll probably die with this lean toward attractional church, but the Holy Spirit is pushing me.

The genius of fresh expressions of church is that it practices a "blended ecology" of both attractional "come to us" and missional "come to you" church. It applies what Jim Collins calls "the genius of the 'and'" as up against "the tyranny of the 'or.'" It also allows both attractional and missional followers of Jesus to cooperate with one another instead of competing with one another.

Missional Field Kit: 50/50 Evaluation

A helpful principle that enables a church to become "God shaped" is the 50/50 principle. On the new missional frontier, local churches need to spend half of their time caring for the existing congregation, and half of their time engaging the larger community. This means half of our time cultivating Jerusalem (traditional, stationary, gathered), and half of our time cultivating Antioch (emerging, mobile, scattered). This principle must be embodied by the senior clergy leader, the staff, and every member of the congregation. Here are two field kit tools to get you started:

Field Kit 1: 50/50 Planner

This is a tool for scheduling days in quarters and mapping out the 50/50.

Step 1. Make a copy of the 50/50 planner for everyone on the team.

Step 2. Designate one day as Sabbath, a 24-hour period (for example, from 5:00 p.m. Thursday to 5:00 p.m. Friday or all day Saturday).

Step 3. Optionally, also designate another day as a day off for work and family.

Step 4. Take the remainder of the work week and fill in the thirds with work. Divide those blocks an even 50/50 between internal work in the church and external work in the community.

Step 5. If you have staff, or a key leadership team, encourage them to do this same exercise with their time.

Step 6. Make these schedules available for the whole congregation. You may even want to designate where you will be in the community on various blocks in the calendar.

Step 7. Encourage everyone in the congregation to restructure their weeks in the same way. How many hours per week do they devote to serving God through the church (after work, school, Sabbath, and so on)? Can they divide those hours in the following way: half spent in service to the traditional congregation, and half spent in service to the larger community? If they are willing, have them turn in their planners.

50-50 PLANNER			
	8AM - 12PM	12PM - 5PM	5PM - 9PM
MON			
TUES			
WED			
THURS			
FRI			
SAT			
SUN			

© 2013 Fresh Expressions US

Field Kit 2: Church-Wide Evaluation

With your church leadership, using the 50/50 planner data, evaluate how much of your weekly time is dedicated to Jerusalem (your inherited congregation) and how much to Antioch (missional engagement with your larger community). Have a conversation about this.

New Field Preachers— Pioneer Ministry

The people called Methodists were born from an evangelism imperative. Not only did the first Methodists adapt to the emerging changes
of society to reach people in the fields, they connected them in a process
of discipleship to journey through the life of grace together. Later, we will
discuss how this process worked in a small-group system in which corresponding ministry constructs existed for each "wave of grace": prevenient
grace (society), justifying grace (class), and sanctifying grace (band). This
imperative required an army of dedicated laity to sustain the movement.

Thus, through solid biblical interpretation, and in some ways through
sheer missional necessity, Wesley affirmed the "priesthood of all believers" and the baptismal vocation of all Christians. Lay persons (men and
women) led the various Methodist gatherings, because they were gifted
by the Spirit for ministry in the church, and as they matured and studied
they became the itinerant preachers.

> Converts were trained to become soul-winners themselves. Many en-
> listed as lay preachers—some itinerant and others local. Many were ap-
> pointed as leaders in their own society, and in addition to watching over
> their own flock, engaged in evangelistic activity in the neighbourhood.[1]

1. Arthur S. Wood, *The Burning Heart: John Wesley, Evangelist* (Minneapolis: Bethany Fellowship, 1978), 194.

One of the most revolutionary features of the Wesleyan revival was its liberation of the laity for leadership, and its blurring of the lines between clergy and lay when it came to priestly functions and spiritual guides. Wesley didn't worry about qualifications since he trusted on-the-job training and expected all Methodists to be lifelong learners.[2]

Some of the factors that stunt Methodist vitality include professionalization of the clergy, lack of leaders indigenous to a particular context, depression of the small-group system, and the diminishment of equipping of the laity for mission. Obviously, lay persons are active in congregations, but in many places their efforts are limited to serving on a committee, leading as a liturgist, or filling in for the preacher a couple of times per year. While these functions were part of lay leadership at a meeting house in Wesley's day, the expectation for mission in the community was paramount. Emerging generations, within reach of the Methodists, also want to be involved in mission, meeting human need, and changing the world. While these future lay leaders may be averse to "membership" or commitment to a single organization, they are more than willing to join in and collaborate with organizations that are making a positive impact in communities.

Time for a Remix

In the global ecosystem, missionary teams are cultivating Jesus communities through the space of flows in a network society. In the Fresh Expressions movement, we label missionaries as "pioneers" because they are particularly adept at moving through the liminality (dislocation, ambiguity) of our age. Three essential roles thrive in the Fresh Expressions movement: pioneers, supporters, and permission givers. This provides a way for every participant (including not-yet-believers) to be involved in

2. Leonard I. Sweet, *The Greatest Story Never Told: Revive Us Again* (Nashville: Abingdon Press, 2012), 79.

mission. When these roles work together in alignment, congregations that have been sedentary for a period can rejoin a movement again.

Pioneers are passionate about mission on the edges.

Supporters are passionate about supporting and releasing pioneers.

Permission Givers are people who use their role to foster release of pioneers and to influence the system to be more willing to experiment.

In the United Kingdom, fresh-expression leaders reorganized the entire ecclesial system to make room for *pioneer ministry*. Persons called by God and gifted by the Spirit for pioneer ministry can do so in a lay, licensed, or ordained capacity.

A clear correlation is observed between pioneer ministers and business or social entrepreneurs. They share essential characteristics. While some are bothered that the term *entrepreneur* is used in business literature, we already use business conceptual language in the church: manager, boards, strategic goals, vitality metrics, quality control, and so on.[3] In *Entrepreneurs: Talent, Temperament and Opportunity*, Bill Bolton and John Thompson define an entrepreneur as "a person who habitually creates and innovates to build something of recognized value around perceived opportunities."[4]

Pioneers share many of these traits: they start new initiatives, organize relational networks, innovate, and create fresh things out of existing pieces. They do so in the power of the Spirit.

The Church of England defines pioneers as "people called by God who are the first to see and creatively respond to the Holy Spirit's initiatives with those outside the church; gathering others around them as they seek to establish a new contextual Christian community."[5]

---

3. David Goodhew, Andrew Roberts, and Michael Volland, *Fresh!: An Introduction to Fresh Expressions of Church and Pioneer Ministry* (London, UK: SCM Press, 2012), 143.

4. Bill Bolton and John Thompson, *Entrepreneurs: Talent, Temperament and Opportunity* (New York: Routledge, 2013), 72.

5. David Male, "Do We Need Pioneers?" 2017. https://freshexpressions.org.uk/get-started /pioneer-ministry/.

The Church of England also identifies two "types" of pioneers, largely based on "from where" the pioneering happens:

- **Fresh-Start Pioneers** (or edge pioneers): These are classic pioneering types who start new things, love firsts, and enjoy working from a blank canvas. If ordained, they need to be released from expectations of an incumbent parish role and allowed to pioneer in places where the Church is not present while remaining closely connected with the diocese.

- **Parish-Based Pioneers** (or mixed-economy pioneers): These pioneers want to work from a parish base but from there develop fresh expressions of church in a mixed economy by expanding the growth and reach of the local church.[6]

As illustrated below, edge pioneers are already out in our communities and we need to join and learn with them. Mixed-economy pioneers are already sitting in our pews and we need to identify and release them.

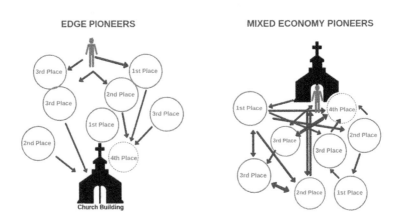

As we find our way through the ambiguity of the current paradigm shift, pioneers function like border-stalkers by moving in and out of the network tribes, bringing hope and reconciliation as they move through

6. Male, "Do We Need Pioneers?"

the different flows and practices. Among the space of flows and the space of places, these border-stalkers don't claim ownership of any sphere among the networks. They empty themselves in the space of the *other* and incarnate God's love within that sphere.[7]

The theological underpinnings of pioneer ministry are rooted deeply in the Trinity. *God is a pioneering God; thus, there are pioneers.* The church is to be one and diverse, in the way the Trinity is one and diverse—distinct persons, living relationally in a mysterious interdependence, full of creative diversity. The relational interpenetration of the Trinity, always making room for the other, is the embodiment of sending, seeking love.

Each person of the Trinity is a "pioneer." As David Goodhew writes in *Fresh!*, God the Father is a pioneer: "God, by the creation of the cosmos, pioneers a new form of reality."[8]

God the Spirit is a pioneer: the Spirit breathes forth all life. Freshness is the hallmark of the Holy Spirit. The Holy Spirit is the "foundation for fresh expressions, pioneer ministry, and church planting." The Holy Spirit is "God as Pioneer Minister—through whom all pioneer ministry finds its authentication and strength." The Spirit "creates community." Thus, the church is a pioneer community of the Spirit.

God the Son is a pioneer: he is the author and instigator of our faith, the one "innovating by who he is (incarnation) what he does (ministry) and by how he dies (cross) and rises again (resurrection)."[9] The Trinity is a pioneer team!

Perhaps the most helpful exercise in our task of understanding and unleashing pioneer ministry comes from the pioneering of Jesus. Hebrews 12:2 (NRSV) reads, "looking to Jesus the *pioneer* and perfecter of our

---

7. *Mearcstapa* (literally, mark-stepper, a boundary walker) or *Border-Stalker* is an Old English term from Beowulf: those who moved between the ancient tribes, living on the edges of their groups, moving in and out, bringing back good news, helping fragmented cultural tribes find hope and reconciliation. Makoto Fujimura, *Culture Care: Reconnecting with Beauty for Our Common Life* (New York: Fujimura Institute, 2014), 39.

8. Goodhew, Roberts, and Volland, *Fresh!*, 25.

9. Goodhew, Roberts, and Volland, *Fresh!*, 24–31.

faith" (italics mine). Here Jesus is identified as the ἀρχηγός (pronounced är-khā-gos), which means "pioneer" or "author" and conversely "instigator." This term is the closest we get in Koiné Greek to "innovator" or "entrepreneur." God bestows the pioneer upon the church for nurture, upbuilding, and expansion. Paul the Apostle is perhaps a textbook example of a pioneer. Pioneers seek to embody this initiator, starter ministry of Jesus in the world. In the same way, we embody the ministry roles of apostle, prophet, evangelist, shepherd, and teacher (Eph 4:11).

Jonny Baker observes that pioneers have "the gift of not fitting in." Pioneers are those who have the uncanny gift to see and imagine different possibilities than the accepted ways of doing business as usual, and then build a path to make real this possibility.[10] This can certainly make them unpopular in more conventional circles.

George Lings reserves the term *pioneer* for "originators of fresh entities," while discussing the differences between pioneer-starters and pioneer-sustainers.[11] In his research, he notes the following characteristics:

- a correlation between apostle and pioneer;
- eagerness to "go first" with low risk-aversion;
- on the "edge," always going out to the edge of some new territory to survey the terrain;
- habitually "create, start, initiate" (which correlates with entrepreneurs);
- draw followers and are followable;
- willing to "leave" (move on when the task is done);
- movers (opposite of static persons);
- "are met by Jesus" (have usually encountered the Risen Christ at some point);
- prefer to be with outsiders;
- at home with "signs" (semioticians, context or sign readers, also embrace the miraculous, and supernatural);
- flexible strategists (employ effectual reasoning, experimentation, improvisation, and intuition);

---

10. Jonny Baker and Cathy Ross, *The Pioneer Gift: Explorations in Mission* (Norwich, UK: Canterbury, 2014), 1.

11. G. Lings, "Looking in the Mirror: What Makes a Pioneer" in David Male, *Pioneers 4 Life: Explorations in Theology and Wisdom for Pioneering Leaders* (Abingdon: Bible Reading Fellowship, 2011), 31.

- Disturb the peace. Some are not easy for more conventional folks to be around because their presence is threatening and difficult for intuitionalists;
- "Bicultural," always formed by and at home in at least two cultures (age, race, nationality, geography, and so on);
- Translators (between times, cultures, peoples, contextual theologians);
- Developers (they activate others and enable them to continue the work);
- Prophetic (they see what is yet unseen and then act: "dreamers who do");
- Can accept suffering and can expect to join Jesus in carrying his cross.[12]

Pioneers often face mutiny, challenges, and cross-carrying. Because of their proclivity to challenge systems and go first in new initiatives, they often do so with arrows in their backs. Most pioneers bear the scars of friendly fire. Three additional characteristics apply to the Fresh Expressions movement:

- Pioneers cultivate fresh expressions (often with little to no resources).
- Pioneers fail forward (fail frequently but keep going).
- Pioneers come in all shapes, sizes, races, and ages; they are not just young, trendy, rebels. (Some pioneers at Wildwood UMC are teens and some are in their eighties.)

T. Hodgett and P. Bradbury, in their research on pioneers from the Church Mission Society, suggest that pioneering needs to be understood as a spectrum:

1. Pioneer innovators: refers to sodal or "sobornistic" pioneer leaders who, with their teams, venture out beyond the edges of the church's structures to explore the creation of faithful expressions of Christian life among people of a new context.

2. Pioneer adaptors: refers to those who have the creative gift to adapt these innovations to their own contexts and take the established church's rituals and rhythms and adapt them into new environments.

---

12. Lings, "Looking in the Mirror," 30–43.

3. Pioneer replicators: refers to those situated in contexts in which replication is applicable, where a context is seen to be sufficiently comparable so that a successful model of church can simply be repeated.

4. Pioneer activists: refers to those whose gift and vocation is to shape a place in ways that seek to align a community, network, or industry with the values of the Kingdom. They see themselves as missionaries but without the express intention of planting a church.[13]

In the following diagram, I have contextualized the pioneer spectrum specifically for the Fresh Expressions US movement, which includes some of our own replicable models: Dinner Church, Church @ Play, and Café Church.

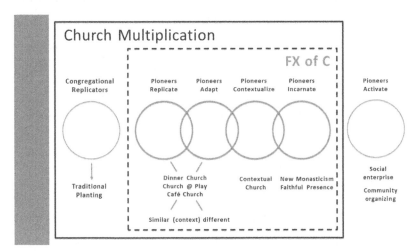

Gerald Arbuckle discusses the reality that though creativity can exist in organizations in a latent way, these ideas require application through innovative people, whom he calls "dreamers who do." He distinguishes between innovators and adaptors:

> Both are creative persons and needed, especially the innovative and refounding type; both threaten the group because they dissent from the

---

13. T. Hodgett and P. Bradbury, "Pioneering Mission is…a spectrum," *ANVIL* 34 no. 1, https://churchmissionsociety.org/resources/pioneering-mission-spectrum-tina-hodgett-paul-bradbury-anvil-vol-34-issue-1/.

acceptable ways of doing things, but it is the innovator that particularly endangers the group's security...[14]

Pioneers can cause a reorganization of the local church. Beth Keith, in "The Gift of Troublesome Questioning," draws a further comparison between adaptors and stabilizers. By their very presence, pioneers threaten overly stable systems by asking "What if?" Stabilizers operate in the impulse to immediately stabilize the disruption. While both have positive and negative attributes, stable systems often support stabilizers only and exile adaptors. Pioneers are gifted by the Spirit to ask troublesome questions that threaten the stability of the system. Pioneers have the ability "to question aspects of the church without drawing the church into question."[15]

Overly stable systems dampen innovation; overly destabilized systems devolve into chaos. Pioneers have a way of destabilizing systems enough to open the organization to the possibility of change. The innovation journey requires some disruption and dissatisfaction. Pioneers are a gift to the church in this way.

Pioneers do not fit neatly into our theological pigeon holes. Their activity and effectiveness challenge the "closely defined liberal, evangelical, or catholic theologies and churchmanship" and they move us "towards something unknown and developmental, with an emphasis on mission, diversity, dialogue and evolving belief and practice."[16]

When intentionally identifying and developing a gifted pioneer, whether in a church, fresh expression, or a formal academic theological setting, consider that pioneers learn in the process of doing, through experimentation and improvisation. Training pipelines are often apprentice-based learning systems. Mature pioneers often possess keen contextual intelligence and become astute contextual theologians, particularly as they

---

14. Gerald A. Arbuckle, *Refounding the Church: Dissent for Leadership* (Maryknoll, NY: Orbis, 1993), 109.

15. B. Keith, "The Gift of Troublesome Questioning" in Male, *Pioneers 4 Life*, 57.

16. Keith, "The Gift of Troublesome Questioning," 56.

gain refined critical-thinking skills that come from depth of education within a particular theological stream.

This can cause denominations to rethink training systems, which usually involve vetting someone theologically and psychologically (by institutional stakeholders) as we let them in and deploy them to congregations. To truly embrace candidates with the pioneer gift, we need to make room in the approval system for them to experiment.

This blending of innovation and sound teaching, driven by the missionary Spirit, challenges some ministry boards, because ministry pioneers tend to have a contextually-formed theology, or a theology shaped through osmosis while living in a different branch on the Christian tree. Pioneers typically struggle before ordination boards, and once included they are often denied seats in decision-making processes. Pioneers are typically not diplomatic and have impatience with the political maneuvers of the institutional church. Because of their "sharp edges" and the "gift of not fitting in," it's easy to write off their questioning or brainstorms as mad ramblings. The Church of England wisely created the Pioneer Assessment Panel, which consists of a group of established pioneers who evaluate incoming pioneers.[17]

The activity of pioneers can create "institutional confusion." The "typical institutional response exhibits stabilizer tendencies and the inability to adapt old data in the light of new experience. The lack of permission to engage in transformative critique may hinder pioneers' abilities to imagine new possibilities."[18] So the tendency then is for the church to select and authorize the "safe" pioneers who will play well with the system, not question common church assumptions, *and* still develop new forms of church. Unfortunately, this is an unreasonable expectation. Thus, denominations often eject the very persons gifted by the Spirit with the adaptation skills that could bring actual revitalization.

---

17. *Vocations to Pioneer Ministry*, https://www.churchofengland.org/pioneering#no-back.

18. Keith, "The Gift of Troublesome Questioning," 58.

There is an ongoing conversation around whether pioneers are born or made. Angela Shier-Jones finds it important to understand a pioneer not as a particular sort of person but as a particular sort of ministerial conduct or focus within the wider framework of the church.[19] All Christians are called to follow the great pioneer, Jesus; this will always include being involved in pioneering. All people created in the image of God have the capacity to start new things. Yet, certain people are particularly gifted to be effective in that particular focus of ministry.

Not all people are pioneers, yet all people can be involved with pioneer ministry. Through creating and leading pioneer academies, I've seen first-hand that pioneers possess a distinct kind of tacit knowledge and naturally display this "ministerial conduct" through a certain set of behaviors or skills. Some disagree with Angela Shier-Jones, arguing that pioneers are indeed a sort of person with inherent characteristics and personality traits that can be identified with sound personality tests.

In my experience, the most prominent trait of a pioneer is simply *confidence.* Pioneers believe they can start new things. They seem gifted to do so. Yet, if pioneering is a gift, it can also be a curse. Hebrews 12:1-2 indicates that when we follow in the slipstream of Jesus's pioneering, enduring a "cross" is par for the course. Further, if everyone were a pioneer, the world would devolve into utter chaos! Can you imagine a church of all adaptors and no stabilizers? Or can you imagine a church where everyone is exactly like Paul? Or if Paul had no Barnabas, a companion encourager (Acts 4:36) who supported him (Acts 9:27), or Ananias, a permission-giver who sent him (Acts 9:17)? So, with fresh expressions, we understand the equal importance of the three roles: pioneer, supporter, and permission-giver.

Perhaps whether pioneers are born or made is the wrong question. Perhaps a more fitting question is *how can we be the church in such a way that every person can be involved in the exciting work of starting new*

---

19. Angela Shier-Jones, *Pioneer Ministry and Fresh Expressions of Church* (London, UK: SPCK, 2009), 3–5.

Christian communities? We find yet another conjunction we must hold in creative tension: every single person can start new things *and* pioneers seem to be especially gifted for this work. This leads us to the more essential truth: pioneer ministry is a work of the body, the whole people of God, and not individual acts of heroic or lone-ranger leadership.

Pioneering is a communal endeavor. Shier-Jones writes, "Pioneering ministry cannot be done to a community by someone who knows what they need; it can only be done with a community by someone who shares in their need."[20] Pioneers are dependent upon the "persons who share peace" and work with the indigenous inhabitants of a community. They must work together with supporters and permission givers in a strategically team-based way, both for the health of the pioneer and the initiatives they start. It's more appropriate to speak of pioneer teams than individual pioneers.

In Download 2, we explored the "space of flows" and the "space of place" in the network society. Physical places serve as "nodes or hubs" in that larger network. So, on this new remixed mission field of a network society, where are the "places" where we can be a "withness"? Where are the missional sandboxes in which pioneer teams play?

The focus on "practices" does not minimize places or people. In fact, the practices and the places are the vehicle through which we form relationships with people. Practices create relational proximity; they enable us to connect in the flows of our mobile social structures. Face-to-face encounter is still the primary place where our isolation is healed. Pioneers raise up indigenous leaders within these communities of practice who in turn raise up more indigenous leaders in the larger web of potential multitudes of networked practices.

Pioneers are focused on planting the seeds of the gospel within the fluidity of these cultural flows, connected by the internet, screens, and social media at the speed of 5G. These encounters take place around shared practices in the first, second, and third places of our larger communal

---

20. Shier-Jones, *Pioneer Ministry and Fresh Expressions of Church*, 123.

ecosystems. One can easily see the potential of this approach, particularly with connecting in the third places around these common hobbies, interests, and bundled practices where they take place.

Here is a refresher:

First Place: The home or primary place of residence.

Second Place: The workplace or school place.

Third Place: The public places separate from the two usual social environments of home and workplace, that "host regular, voluntary, informal, and happily anticipated gatherings of individuals...." Examples are environments such as cafes, pubs, clubs, parks, and so on.[21]

Towns, workplaces, and hobbies exist in a complex web of networked micro-communities. Technology connects people across geographic spaces among those who share common passions. Long ago, community decoupled from locality; it is now centered around leisure, work, and friendships. Technology is now harnessed to connect people in networks, and mobility allows for those networks to transcend locality.

Fresh expressions have tremendous potential in third places. The concept of first, second, and third places was developed by sociologist Ray Oldenburg. Third places are physical, public locations where local residents informally gather to converse with each other. He posited that third places were unique from other public venues because they were places of informal conversation.

From *The Great Good Place*, here's a summarization of the shared characteristics of Oldenburg's third place:

Neutral Ground—Individuals may come and go as they please, no one is forced to "play the host." Thus, individuals can visit without out a sense of obligation.

---

21. Ray Oldenburg, *The Great Good Place: Cafés, Coffee Shops, Bookstores, Bars, Hair Salons, and Other Hangouts at the Heart of a Community* (New York: Marlowe, 1999), 16.

Leveler—Reduces everyone in the space to a shared equality regardless of rank or class. It's an inclusive atmosphere, typified by downward association in an uplifting manner, where social strata distinctions are leveled; rich and poor, king and pauper, commune as equals.

Conversational—The atmosphere is informal. Jovial discourse is the main activity.

Accessibility—People can easily access the place beyond normal working hours. Third places often keep late or early hours. Also, they are typically proximally close to the first and second places of our normal rhythms. Proximity and convenience are keys to this accessibility.

Regulars—The grassroots community forms among fellow patrons, not something management provides. The regulars provide the sense of conviviality. Like in the television show *Cheers*, it's a place "where everybody knows your name."

Low Profile—The physical space does not refocus attention away from interpersonal communication. The focus is on relaxation and support that fosters feelings of acceptance.

Playful—The persistent mood is one of playfulness. Leave your overly serious attitude at the door.

Home—This place glows with the warmth of home, it truly becomes a home away from home.[22]

The church once embodied the accessibility and neutrality central to third places in many US communities. In some rural locations, this is still the case. But across the North American landscape, the church largely no longer exists as a third place for the surrounding neighborhoods. For emerging generations, the church is another kind of secret-society lodge, where a peculiar group of people gather to enact strange rituals and use

---

22. Oldenburg, *The Great Good Place*, 20–40.

coded language. For many, it is not a viable space to gather and form community.

While in some sense the beauty of a third place has become lost in the relentless work-anxiety cycle of our postmodern culture, understanding how mobile human community forms regularly in these places is essential to our missional task. The formation of community around practices, if albeit sometimes momentarily, is indeed the space of places where pioneers play.

The power of harnessing these third places to form communal life with Jesus is evidenced by the diversity of fresh expressions emerging among the wide array of common practices that take place in accessible, neutral, inclusive, conversational, spaces. As we saw earlier, practices may include tattooing, yoga, kayaking, running, burritos, pets, coffee, tai chi, and the list goes on ad infinitum!

However, to be clear, fresh expressions of church are not merely about places or practices; they are about people: love of people. The guiding questions are not: Do I love this place? Do I love this practice? The questions are: Do I love "the regulars" of this place? Do I love the people who participate in this practice? Rather than asking, Do I love burritos? ask, Do I love the people who love burritos? Not, Do I love tattooing? but, Do I love the people who find tattooing to be the external artistic expression of their inner lives? Not simply, Do I love yoga? but, Do I love the people who practice yoga that may or may not have any connection with the church?

This is a remixed form of McGavran's "people movement" discussed earlier, but it is centered on these communal practices. Bolger defines "practice movements" as a missional approach that focuses on the activities that bind people to each other in time and space (i.e., practices). Place becomes secondary to the social space of connections enabled by microelectronics-based information and communications technologies. Diverse peoples flow in and out of practice-centered communities. These movements involve pioneering Christ-followers who engage these practices through establishing an incarnational presence within the common community.[23]

So then, fresh expressions live in a continual tension of openness to others and a radical call to discipleship. They exist primarily as "centered-set" communities which practice belonging before believing.

We noticed at Wildwood that many people who connected with us in our fresh expressions of church would eventually visit our Sunday morning services. Many also didn't return. So, for the blended ecology to work, we needed to create a "fourth place." This is a space in between a fresh expression and a traditional form of church. It's a soft place to land for "nones and dones" who wanted to experience a more traditional form of church. For Wildwood, we call that space "New Life," which is discussed in detail later. Here's a vision of how pioneer teams move through the spheres, bringing others along on the journey:

THE BLENDED ECOLOGY ECOSYSTEM

How Pioneers Move Through the Five Spheres

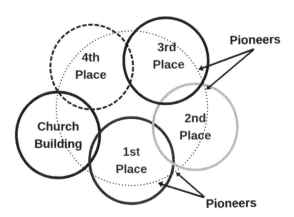

23.   Ryan K. Bolger, "Practice Movements in Global Information Culture: Looking Back to McGavran and Finding a Way Forward," *Missiology* 35, no. 2: 181–93 (2007), 189–90.

Notice the distinction of the lines in the diagram, both light and dark, solid and broken; this is a distinction between "bounded" and "centered" sets. In a bounded-set, a community has clear boundaries, established around beliefs and behaviors, which are patrolled and enforced. One is included or excluded based on adherence. In a centered-set, a community is comprised of non-negotiable core convictions, which are enthusiastically supported and maintained. While an inclusive community, the core convictions shape behavior. One is free to explore moving toward the center, regardless of where in proximity they may be to those beliefs and behaviors.[24]

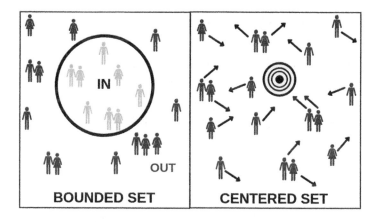

Fresh expressions of church, and particularly the fourth place, operate in a "centered-set" way, rather than as a "bounded-set." They are communities that primarily follow a "belonging before believing" journey.[25] In a blended-ecology ecosystem, both bounded and centered sets are valuable. The blended-ecology church harnesses the power of both.

Then how do we identify and release pioneers in the missional ecosystems of the local church? If Jonny Baker is correct, and pioneers have "the gift of not fitting in," they will be easy to spot. Shier-Jones, in

---

24. Stuart Murray, *Church after Christendom* (Milton Keynes: Paternoster, 2004), 28–31.

25. Murray, *Church after Christendom*, 71.

distinguishing between pioneer ministers and traditional ministers, notes that "they may well present as aggressive, pushy, intense, charismatic and bold rather than accessible, pastoral, supportive, and 'nice.'"[26] In fact, pioneers "smell each other." Pioneers spot other pioneers, and they form strategic partnerships quickly.

You will know pioneers "by their love" or perhaps whom they love, how they initiate community with those they love, and by how they think.

First, a key characteristic of pioneers is that they prefer to be with outsiders. They seem to love outsiders more than insiders. They always have their eyes out for the "other," those who are not "in" yet. Who in your church still has one foot in the world? This person is passionate about a certain people, place, or practice outside the church. He or she misses church functions because of hobbies, or belonging to a club, or gathering with others to participate in a practice. That person could be a pioneer.

Second, pioneers start stuff. Quite honestly, this separates pioneers from wannabes. They have a track record of initiating new things. For example, perhaps this began with lemonade stands in childhood, monetizing new ideas with elementary school classmates, which led to start-up companies, creating new worship services, or harnessing technology to start groups or clubs. It is in a pioneer's nature to initiate. While some people are holding meetings about launching new ventures, pioneers are out launching new ventures. Fledgling pioneers can be dizzying to work with because they are always moving on to the next big idea, the next exciting opportunity, often prematurely. As pioneers mature, they learn to work through teams and help communities value and adopt their ideas. They learn to create cultural change, and form communities of settlers who sustain their innovations.

Third, pioneers literally think differently. They employ the effectual reasoning typical of entrepreneurs. The word *effectual* is the inverse of *causal*. Causal rationality starts with a pre-determined goal and seeks to

---

26. Shier-Jones, *Pioneer Ministry and Fresh Expressions of Church,* 122.

develop strategic steps toward meeting that goal. Effectual reasoning does not start with a specific goal. Rather, it begins with a given reality and "allows goals to emerge contingently over time from the varied imagination and diverse aspirations of the founders and the people they interact with."[27]

Classic Causation Model from Marketing Textbooks

Process of Effectuation Used by Expert Entrepreneurs

For instance, while causal reasoning focuses on expected return, effectual reasoning emphasizes affordable loss; causal reasoning depends upon competitive analyses, effectual reasoning is built upon strategic partnerships; causal reasoning urges the exploitation of pre-existing knowledge and prediction, effectual reasoning stresses the leveraging of contingencies.[28]

Thus, by taking the "effects" and starting with who and what pioneers already have, they begin to create something new from the pieces.

27. Saras D. Sarasvathy, "What Makes Entrepreneurs Entrepreneurial?" https://www.effectuation.org/sites/default/files/documents/what-makes-entrepreneurs-entrepreneurial-sarasvathy.pdf, 2.

28. Sarasvathy, "What Makes Entrepreneurs Entrepreneurial?" 2.

Through a series of relational interactions, as opportunities and strategic partnerships arise, multiple outcomes are possible. This kind of reasoning often employed by pioneers and entrepreneurs can fuel a journey of innovation in a traditional congregation.

Who in your community has a history of starting things? Who is always initiating, creating, or having big ideas about what could be? Who is consistently asking troublesome "what if" questions that rattle the guardians of the status quo?

While revitalization begins with a community of leaders in the inherited church, those leaders will need to begin cultivating the emerging forms of church in the community. In the blended ecology, every member can be involved in pioneer ministry; every pioneer team has the capacity to be church planters.

Jorge mentioned earlier the work of Alan Hirsch and the concept of fivefold ministry or APEST (Apostles, Prophets, Evangelists, Shepherds, Teachers) from Ephesians 4:11-13. Hirsch and others in the missional church movement call for the "recalibration" of the church in the West, explaining how a return to the fivefold ministry as a "primordial form" (one of the meta-ideas that serves as a foundational concept) is essential for the multiplication of the church.[29]

Every church needs persons with all five APEST characteristics, to mature to its fullest potential. Fresh expressions give us a process to live this out by releasing the whole priesthood of all believers to plant new forms of church. This is a new generation of bold itinerant field preachers—Methodism remixed for the emerging missional frontier. Pioneers, alongside supporters and permission givers, do this work together. Along with hiring professional church planters, we may need to recognize we have some already in our pews or just outside the walls within our communal sphere of influence.

---

29.   Alan Hirsch, *5Q: Reactivating the Original Intelligence and Capacity of the Body of Christ* (USA: 100M, 2017), 19.

Managerial Thinking -- Causal Reasoning

Distinguishing Characteristic:

Selecting between given means to achieve a pre-determined goal

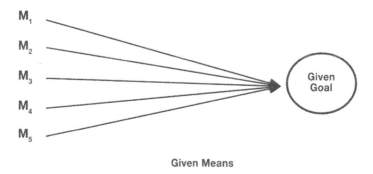

Given Means

Entrepreneurial Thinking -- Effectual Reasoning

Distinguishing Characteristic:

Imagining possible new ends using a given set of means

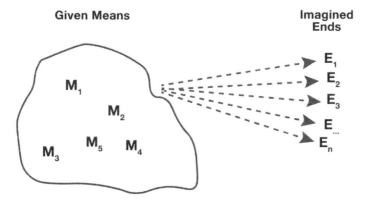

Blended-ecology pioneers are both/and people; they are border stalkers. However, let's not fall into the misconception that pioneers are solo acts; mature pioneers understand that pioneering is a work of the body. They not only initiate new things, they organize relational networks to sustain their innovations. Who in your congregation or community exemplifies these characteristics? You need those persons on your team.

Field Story—Beck

Several years ago, a nearby United Methodist mega-church planted a second site in a community center less than a mile away from our church facility. Some of our people were deeply afraid and threatened. They were also gripped with resentment toward our episcopal leadership and conference. "Why would they plant that church there? Do they want us to die? Why don't they care about us anymore?"

We live on the edge of The Villages, a retirement community for people age fifty-five and older, and one of the fastest-growing cities in Florida. The concern of the congregation is seemingly valid on a surface level. People who moved into the area could have potentially joined our church (although many Villagers insist on and enjoy a certain status in attending a church within The Villages, with golf cart accessibility). Further, Villagers and Wildwood members have a tense relational history.

I began to assure our congregation not to be concerned with this new church being planted in our backyard. The mission field is bigger than any amount of people our churches can faithfully engage. Many falsely assume that Villagers, who are in the later stages of life, will automatically go to church. They are "studying for the final" so to speak, so they must want to make sure they are right with God, correct? Not the case. Most Village residents do not regularly attend church. The Boomer generation is retiring, and even some Gen Xers are beginning to retire. Those generations abandoned the inherited church in large numbers. This is a big mission field.

Another reason to side-step concern is that perceiving another church as a competitive threat is small-minded Christendom thinking. Not only are other churches *not* our enemy, we are on the same team! This is kingdom thinking. John Wesley joined with fellow Christians across the theological spectrum to focus on the mission of God. In pioneer language, this is about "strategic partnerships."

I reached out to the pastor of this church plant, Rev. Jim Divine and he has become a true friend. He is an incredible leader: humble, gifted, and unabashedly focused on the mission of Jesus Christ. He thinks at a kingdom level, not a self-interested institutional church level. This mindset is partly why this satellite congregation grew from zero to a thousand very quickly. One day, in conversation among our leaders, we decided to combine our fresh expressions teams. Each of the churches has its own unique set of challenges.

In a smaller, one-hundred-forty-year-old church, I face the continuous challenges of finding resources, sustaining worn-out properties, watching precious saints graduate into the new creation, and conducting dozens of funerals every year. However, a small old church also has some advantages. We have the "gift of desperation," so we can take risks much more easily. We don't have nearly the level of bureaucracy and politics found in a larger church. We have the capacity to make decisions quickly—ideally, although not always in practice. We have been able to cultivate fresh expressions with a seeming degree of ease in our community.

Through cultivating fresh expressions, our church experienced renewed life, since a network of fifteen fresh expressions is like a microdistrict of multi-site churches. This also frees the pastor to be in the community connecting with people, harnessing the emerging technologies in networks. In fact, this new kind of multi-site scenario is creating a new definition for "mega-church pastor"—those who have "small" congregations in the *space of place.* For instance, I am appointed quarter-time as a pastor of Wildwood UMC. Yet in my national role, I "pastor" many thousands of people throughout the United States, especially through the technologically enabled *space of flows*, and from my various social media platforms. It is possible that a new breed of mega-church pastor does indeed have a reach much larger in scope than a traditional brick and mortar mega-church in the network society. I am more mobile and the expectations on my time are much lower than a pastor in a traditional mega-church scenario.

The challenges in the large church are quite different: bureaucracy with red tape and many meetings, navigating the politics, and massive debt on new construction. High expectations are placed upon a large-church pastor's time, and much of it involves the office and inherited church work. However, a large church also has some advantages: an army of people power, a brand-new building, a steady stream of visitors moving into the area by the thousands, and tremendous financial resources.

However, Jim, a large-church pastor who also likes starting fresh expressions, is not your typical pastor. To be effective, it takes a vile, field-preaching kind of Methodist. It's not enough to sit back and wait for people to come visit the shiny new building. His effective satellite church lives in a blended ecology of inherited and emerging forms. The entrepreneurs down the road from us are one of the few mega-churches that have a fresh expressions team and are equally committed to attractional *and* missional forms of church.

At one point, the large church was stuck. They were having lots of meetings, operating within the bureaucracy of a larger church, following protocol, checking all the boxes. They were carefully planning everything before they started. Yet they weren't actually starting many fresh expressions! At our first collective meeting between our two teams, we led them through the Marshmallow Tower Challenge. We split our teams up in groups of four to six people and gave each team twenty sticks of dry spaghetti, one yard of string, one yard of tape, one marshmallow, and a measuring tape. We told them to build the tallest tower possible in eighteen minutes that would support the marshmallow. We set a timer and then go—just do it!

At the end of the time, we measured each team's structure. Some teams had nothing to measure! Some towers dropped, limping down to the table before we could measure. We asked each team to describe their process and share what they learned. Then we showed them this TED Talk from Tom Wujec: https://www.ted.com/talks/tom_wujec_build_a_tower.

The purpose of the challenge is to encourage a design-thinking mindset and create team synergy. With the simple ingredients and eighteen minutes, your team must build the tallest possible tower under tremendous pressure. Most teams spend much of their time planning before they start building. The best marshmallow tower builders in the world are kindergarteners. They don't have a committee meeting; they just start experimenting and building with unlimited creativity. Primarily the exercise forces teams to build through repeated iterations—failing forward faster. We led the teams to process the experience together in order to illustrate how to shift into an experimental, people-centered, fresh expressions approach.

Fresh expressions are micro-experiments and typically don't work by scheduling a series of planning meetings, which often proliferate because the leaders are afraid to make the wrong decision if large financial risks are at stake. By using effectual reasoning, pioneers take what they have (people, resources, ideas, relationships, places) and they start. They take the pieces and build something new. They begin and figure it out as they go, rather than figuring it all out and then starting.

Our teams had one planning meeting, then started our first collaborative fresh expression a week later: breakfast church with kids in the Martin Luther King Jr. Building. (For more information, see the Field Story for Download 10.) We had almost fifty people show up for the first gathering, many of whom had no connection with either of our churches.

We have learned that when churches can move beyond the fear of protecting territory, catch a kingdom vision, and collaborate, then amazing things can happen. Fresh expressions give us a vehicle for working together. Smaller churches with the incentive from desperation and little to risk but with long-term relationships in a community can partner with larger churches and their resources. These churches can learn together and harness the power of our connectionalism. They can complement each other's weaknesses.

There are more "people fish" in the sea (Matt 4:18-22) than we can catch and release together, much less in isolation. Our focus is not about reaching the already Christians playing churchy musical chairs. We are focused on reaching not-yet-Christians. We are not attempting to get them back in our respective church compounds either. We are focused on being church with them where they are. This is something all churches can do by partnering together for the kingdom harvest in which the "harvest is plentiful, but the laborers are few" (Luke 10: 2 NRSV).

Missiography—"Come, Holy Spirit. Come." (Acevedo)

I was not raised Methodist but was grafted into the Wesleyan family in the late 1970s. Rescued by Jesus a few days before my eighteenth birthday, I landed in a United Methodist Church not knowing anything about the rich heritage of the Methodist movement. I honestly started attending Pine Castle United Methodist Church because they had an awesome student and college ministry filled with beautiful young women. I married one of those women, and thirty-seven years later we are still crazy in love with each other.

Only during college and later in seminary did I learn about the rich history and robust theology of this apostolic movement led by John Wesley and his band of missionaries in the 1700s. Three moments happened with John Wesley, sparking the apostolic, missionary movement known as Methodism. They happened between May of 1738 and April of 1739.

The first was John Wesley's "heartwarming" experience at Aldersgate on May 24, 1738. He wrote in his journal these words:

I felt my heart strangely warmed. I felt I did trust in Christ, Christ alone, for salvation; and an assurance was given me that He had taken away my sins, even mine, and saved me from the law of sin and death.[30]

Many have argued that this was his salvation moment. Others disagree. Clearly, he experienced the assurance of his salvation. Something "clicked" in Mr. Wesley that he was indeed a forgiven child of God. It was a game changer for him.

The second of John Wesley's experiences in those ten and a half months happened early in the morning of Monday, January 1, 1739. The evening before, the last day of 1738, he set out to a prayer meeting. He wrote in his journal:

> About three in the morning, as we were continuing instant in prayer, the power of God came mightily upon us insomuch that many cried out for exceeding joy and many fell to the ground.[31]

Mr. Wesley had a Pentecostal experience, a supernatural encounter with the Holy Spirit that evening at Fetter Lane.

The third experience occurred over several days in Bristol, a seaport city in England. On Saturday, March 31, 1739, Wesley wrote in his journal:

> In the evening I reached Bristol and met Mr. Whitefield there. I could scarcely reconcile myself at first to this strange way of preaching in the fields, of which he set me an example on Sunday; I had been all my life (till very lately) so tenacious of every point relating to decency and order that I should have thought the saving of souls almost a sin if it had not been done in a church.[32]

---

30. *Journal of John Wesley*, May 24, 1738.

31. *Journal of John Wesley*, January 1, 1739.

32. *Journal of John Wesley*, March 31, 1739.

His hesitancy about field preaching is understandable given his formal training as an Anglican priest. But two days later on Monday, April 2, 1739, Wesley described what he did:

> At four in the afternoon, I submitted to be more vile and proclaimed in the highways the glad tidings of salvation.[33]

Field preaching at Bristol became his "defining moment" in terms of a missional, fresh expression of church among a people who were unlikely to attend the attractional, inherited church. This strategy served the fledging Methodist movement well as new people were reached in new places.

It is somewhat risky to ground theology around a personal narrative, but (from the perspective of "ecclesiology") it is correct to say that John Wesley's Aldersgate experience of assurance added to his Fetter Lane encounter with the Holy Spirit laid the tracks for discovering a new strategy for pioneer ministry at Bristol. Sadly, far too often I have, as a Christian leader, tried to lead an innovative, Spirit-led, apostolic missional ministry without moments of assurance about my salvation and fresh encounters with the Holy Spirit. I must honestly confess that in over three decades of ministry I have been there too often. So, join me in praying, "Come, Holy Spirit. Come."

Missional Field Kit
Interest Surveys:
Identifying and Releasing Pioneers

To cultivate fresh expressions from the base of the local church, we need pioneers.

One way to identify these people is simply to survey what interests, hobbies, and practices the people in our relational spheres may participate in each week. What do they do for fun, recreation, and community? Later

---

33. *Journal of John Wesley*, April 2, 1739.

we will help give some suggestions for how those practices can become forms of church.

Prepare a survey or bulletin announcement or email, with the following four simple questions:

1. A pioneer is someone capable of taking the church outside the walls and who can relate or interact with the people there. Do you consider yourself a pioneer, and if so, are you willing to serve on our team?

2. What are your hobbies, interests, or passions—that is, what do you love to do in your spare time?

3. What "networks" of people outside the church are you involved with? What groups do you participate in (for example, quilting, golf, fitness, bingo, clubs, civic organizations, communities, and so on)?

4. What places do you frequent every week? Where do you like to hang out?

Remember that pioneers come in all shapes, sizes, ages, and colors. With your team, have a conversation about the survey results and start recruiting.

See a sample survey on the following page.

90

DOWNLOAD 5

Masterpiece beneath the Mess—A Journey of Grace

While John Wesley urged us to understand our disease, which is original sin, remarkably, the starting point for Wesley's understanding of salvation is a humanity created in the image of God and called "very good."

At Wildwood, I once preached a sermon titled "Masterpiece beneath the Mess" to flesh out a Wesleyan understanding of salvation. Standing before the congregation on an easel was what appeared to be a framed art piece, totally obscured with washable paint. I asked the congregation, "What if I told you that beneath this mess was the most valuable masterpiece ever created? More valuable than Raphael's *Sistine Madonna* or Michelangelo's *Creation of Adam*, or any da Vinci, Monet, or Picasso ever made? What if I told you that I knew a master of restoration who could heal any masterpiece? Even this mess." I then began to share from Genesis about the "very good" nature of God's creation, of which human beings are "supremely good" among all created things (Gen 1:27-31). Human beings are fundamentally relational beings, created to live in loving relationship with our triune God.

In "The New Creation" Wesley stated, "there will be a deep, an intimate, an uninterrupted union with God; a constant communion with

91

Father, Son, and Holy Spirit." [1] To be a "new creation" or enter "heaven" is to enjoy an unbroken relationship with God. In fact, the vision of new creation is a remix of the first creation. Humanity already enjoyed this relationship. In God's vulnerable love, God created humanity with the ability to choose or reject God's relational nature. Humanity exercised this gift called free will in the wrong direction, severed that relationship, and unleashed devastating consequences on all of creation (Gen 3). Thus, the *imago Dei* (image of God) became marred, broken, and obscured by sin.

In his day, Wesley confronted a group of what he called "gospel preachers" whose message was similar to what we might call the "prosperity gospel." He says these so-called gospel preachers

> corrupt their hearers; they vitiate their taste, so that they cannot relish sound doctrine; and spoil their appetite, so they cannot turn it into nourishment; they, as it were, feed them with sweetmeats, till the genuine wine of the kingdom seems quite insipid to them. They give them cordial upon cordial, which make them all life and spirit for the present; but meantime their appetite is destroyed, so they can neither retain nor digest the pure milk of the Word. Hence it is that (according to the constant observation I have made in all parts both of England and Ireland) preachers of this kind (though quite the contrary it seems at first), spread death, not life, among their hearers.[2]

A mutant Wesleyan "prosperity gospel," in which the preaching or teaching is more like self-help therapy, is prevalent in many congregations today. This perspective doesn't take the human condition seriously. John Wesley lists the three essential beliefs of Methodism succinctly as "original sin, justification by faith alone, and holiness of heart and life." [3] Thus the Methodist understanding of humanity requires holding four key concepts

---

1. John Wesley, "The New Creation," *The Standard Sermons in Modern English*, ed. K. C. Kinghorn (Nashville, 2002), 102.

2. John Wesley, et al., *The Works of John Wesley* (Nashville: Abingdon Press, 1984), *Letters*, Vol. III, "To Ebenezer Blackwell, 20 December, 1751," 84.

3. William H. Willimon, *United Methodist Beliefs: A Brief Introduction* (Louisville, KY: Westminster John Knox, 2007), 13.

in tension: creation, sin, grace, and law. Grace is the center of our doctrine. It begins with the grace of creation, "very good." Yet, that original goodness is fractured, and saving grace becomes necessary in relation to inbeing sin.[4] Charles Wesley sings "Take away our *bent* to sinning" (italics mine).[5] We are warped, bent, and in a sense deformed by sin. We are in need of redemption, a redemption we cannot accomplish for ourselves. We need to be re-formed from our sin-bent state. Thus, we need grace. Furthermore, we need a savior: God incarnate in Jesus Christ.

Through outreach, recovery ministries, and fresh expressions of our church, I am continually engaged with not-yet-Christians, "dones," as well as folks from other denominations. I've encountered differing ideas about what "salvation" actually is. Our grace-centered United Methodist perspective is distinct; God's love manifests in waves of grace. While not divided, grace is experienced in various stages, if you will.[6] First, God's relational love is seeking us, calling out "Where are you?" (Gen 3:9). Arguing against Pelagius, Saint Augustine speaks of "preventing" grace, that the first move in salvation is initiated by God.[7] Wesley drew from Augustine here. Preceding conscious awareness, God is after us, relentlessly pursuing us, protecting us. Realizing that great love then moves us to accept our brokenness and engage God's transforming grace (Rom 2:4; 1 John 4:19).

The entire "way of salvation" reveals our Wesleyan theological thrust toward what Maddox calls "responsible grace."[8] God wants to restore us fully to the divine image, God's pre-fall masterpiece, and enable us to completely love God and neighbor. Yet, this does not occur passively. Our

4. Randy Maddox, *Responsible Grace: John Wesley's Practical Theology* (Nashville: Kingswood, 1994), 75.

5. "Love Divine, All Loves Excelling," no. 384, *United Methodist Hymnal*, stanza 2.

6. Scott Jones, *United Methodist Doctrine: The Extreme Center* (Nashville: Abingdon Press, 2002), 148.

7. Saint Augustine in *Documents of the Christian Church* (Oxford: Oxford University Press, 1999), 60.

8. Maddox, *Responsible Grace*, 83.

life becomes a lived "response" to God's grace. Our development requires some faith work on our part. As James reminds us, faith is dead when it doesn't result in faithful activity (Jas 2:17). Wesley believed this movement along the "way of salvation" marks our lives in a special way. We grow in both personal and social holiness along this journey of grace through the "means of grace."

Our identity as Christians necessitates belonging to a community of accountable discipleship.[9] The true genius of the early Methodist movement was not only reaching people in the "fields" but inviting them into an intentional discipleship process that helped them along the journey of grace.

John Wesley believed that entire sanctification, perfection in love, is achievable in this life. Love of God and neighbor is the ultimate goal but it cannot be accomplished in isolation. It was the genius of the small groups that helped create a system in which people could journey in the power of the Spirit through the life of grace. Methodists with their lives now ripe with the fruit of the Spirit (Gal 5:22-23), could bear the marks of an authentic Christian life, including faith, hope, and love (1 Cor 13:13).[10]

As I concluded the "Masterpiece Beneath the Mess" sermon, I used a rag to wipe away the junk that was obscuring the masterpiece below. As I wiped away the covering paint, I described the process of restoration. I emphasized our Wesleyan understanding of grace manifesting in primarily three waves. God's prevenient grace is calling us, wooing us, meeting us in the mess, never giving up. Christ's atoning work makes available the justifying grace, which redeems us and begins our regeneration. Then, by sanctifying grace, the Spirit is continually restoring us into the very fullness of God's image. As the shiny, mirrored surface began to appear, I lifted up not a piece of framed art but a mirror.

The listeners beheld their faces in the reflection as I walked among the congregation. I explained that each of us has also been obscured, marred

---

9. Dietrich Bonhoeffer, *Life Together* (New York: Harper & Row, 1954), 21.

10. Jones, *United Methodist Doctrine,* 202.

by the consequences of sin (Gen 6:5; Rom 3:10, 23; Isa 64:6). Just like that mirror, we are powerless to remove the junk for ourselves. If we understood that every life was a priceless masterpiece of God in the graceful process of restoration, perhaps it would help us truly love. Jesus is our healer, lovingly wiping away the confusion, the chaos, and the clutter. The Spirit is continually polishing us into Christ's image throughout our lives (Rom 8:29).

Time for a Remix

The creative starting point of our missional posture in fresh expressions is "supremely good." We believe "goodness" is baked into every layer of creation and every person within it. Like a cake, the fundamental ingredients of God's universe are epic goodness, beauty, and truth of massive proportions. We get to go on a treasure hunt in our communities to identify and play forth these ingredients, showcasing them for all to taste. We search for the beauty, truth, and goodness already there, and collaborate with God in their cultivation. This profound goodness is also in every person, yet sometimes we need to look harder. God is already present in every place and every individual where we go. And yet, there are other forces at work as well.

Early in my own ministry I became a student of Jorge Acevedo at Grace. Grace Church has one of the strongest Celebrate Recovery (CR) programs in the nation and has now created their own contextually faithful variation called Choose Recovery. One of the many things I admire about Choose Recovery is that it forces us to acknowledge that every human being is in recovery—from sin. Not all of us suffer from the diseases that show up as addictions, but each of us has a sinful condition that manifests in the various ways we try to fill our whole being with food, sex, work, control, approval, and so on.[11]

---

11. Gayle Felton, quoting H. G. Wells as speaking of the "God-shaped blank" in every person in *United Methodists and the Sacraments* (Nashville: Abingdon Press, 2007), 12.

These substitutions for God's presence are the symptoms of an underlying disease. As a missionary pastor, I'm often brought face-to-face with the depths of brokenness and the need for grace. Every time I watch a couple divorce for marital unfaithfulness, witness the desperation of a person who seemingly can't stop drinking, hear the confession of a longtime Christian hooked on pornography, or work with parents who abandoned their children in the midst of their drug use, I see this need for grace. In many instances, I have seen God work in miraculous and reconciling ways.

In a post-Christian society, discussions about "sin" and the "cross" can shut down acknowledgment of grace. Bad Christians happen to good people, and "bad theology" runs rampant around us. The damage is apparent when helping an individual recognize God's reconciling love. Some Christians and seekers struggle with the concept of God's redemption through "sacrifice." By analogy, Martin Luther King Jr. reminds us that "violence merely increases hate.... Darkness cannot drive out darkness, only light can do that."[12]

Historically, four primary models of atonement explain how Jesus's sacrifice reconciles us to God. The *Christus victor* model emphasizes a cosmic battle taking place between good and evil on the cross. This model holds that through the crucifixion and resurrection of Jesus, the powers of death and evil binding humanity were ultimately defeated. The *moral example* model describes Jesus's death as an example of God's self-sacrificial love, which inspires humanity to love accordingly. The *satisfaction* model maintains that sin was an affront to God's justice. Hence, Jesus stepped in as a substitute on behalf of sin-ridden humanity. The *penal-substitutionary* model highlights that God imputed the guilt of our sins onto Jesus, and Jesus received our punishment in our stead.[13]

---

12. *Where Do We Go from Here?* (Boston: Beacon, 1967), 67.

13. Shirley C. Guthrie, *Christian Doctrine* (Louisville, KY: Westminster John Knox, 1994), 252–60.

Each of these models has strengths and weaknesses, yet with unintended consequences contribute to an ideology of violence. One way to reframe this dilemma is captured powerfully by Dan Bell: "God does not demand blood . . . we do."[14] Jesus is the fullness of God's beauty, truth, and goodness—enfleshed. The life of heaven comes to earth, not simply as a satisfaction or substitution but as God's pure, nonviolent, unbounded love—and we give him hell. Thomas Aquinas said, "the greatest offence was perpetrated in the passion of Christ, since his slayers committed the most grievous of sins."[15] Jesus's death ends all need for violence. The cross is ultimately a way God engages our sin and suffering. Charles Wesley proclaims, "God for me hath died: my Lord, my love, is crucified!"[16] As S. Mark Heim states, "Redemptive violence is our equation. Jesus didn't volunteer to get into God's justice machine. God volunteered to get into ours. God used our own sin to save us."[17]

Jürgen Moltmann helps navigate this by centering our understanding of atonement in the Trinity. He discusses the cross not only in a soteriological sense, but from a trinitarian framework we are reminded that Jesus the Son is also God. The crucified Christ is the "crucified God," not simply a moment of transaction between the two.[18] Furthermore, it is not only the cross that is redemptive, all of Jesus's life and death are imperative for our redemption. Saint Athanasius articulates, "God became like us [human] so that we might become like God."[19] The resurrection demonstrates the completed work of redemption and total atonement (Rom 1:4). Christ's atonement is not the entirety of Christ's work; it's the foundation for his

---

14. See Dan Bell in D. B. Laytham, *God Does Not Entertain, Play "Matchmaker," Hurry, Demand Blood, Cure Every Illness* (Grand Rapids, MI: Brazos, 2009), 58.

15. Aquinas in *Documents of the Christian Church* (Oxford: Oxford University Press, 1999), 161.

16. "O Love Divine, What Hast Thou Done," no. 287, *United Methodist Hymnal*, stanza 4.

17. *Saved from Sacrifice: A Theology of the Cross* (Grand Rapids, MI: Eerdmans, 2006), xi.

18. *The Crucified God: The Cross of Christ as the Foundation and Criticism of Christian Theology.* (Minneapolis: Fortress, 1993), 201–2.

19. Athanasius, *On the Incarnation* (Crestwood, NY: St. Vladimir's Seminary Press, 1993), 55.

present work as the Risen Lord. Hence, God's grace transforms our lives through a personal relationship with Jesus and the infilling of the Holy Spirit.

Every generation seems to manifest a distinct form of sin-bentness. The pervading struggle of our time is shame: a painful feeling of humiliation or distress caused by a conscious sense of not-enough-ness. Shame is a self-worth issue, in which we question the value of our own personhood. When young people share openly about their struggles in fresh expressions of church, the conversation usually leans toward shame. In the super-competitive nature of a consumerist society, where the "winners" are idolized, the rest of us are the losers. Those of us who don't possess super-model beauty, immense wealth, or genius intelligence, can develop a mentality of deficiency. The network society floods us with global images of success and wealth, perfectly filtered and Instagram-worthy. This is a breeding ground for shame.

Perhaps we need a new theory of reconciliation for the network society, the *Jesus Antivirus Model.* Think of it as a "divine defrag" of the virus-infected hard drive of the universe. Sin causes fragmentation at every level of creation: fragmentation in our relationships with God, each other, and to creation itself. This breech leads us to acknowledge in our hyper-individualism that something is lacking. Shame pushes us into isolation. Jesus incarnates himself in the virus-ridden network, in a specific "node" called Nazareth (space of place). Like anti-virus software, Jesus draws the virus infecting the system into one location, concentrated in his own body on the cross: "He carried in his own body on the cross the sins we committed. He did this so that we might live in righteousness, having nothing to do with sin. By his wounds you were healed" (1 Pet 2:24).

The "rulers and authorities" gather collectively at the cross and are "disarmed" and triumphed over in a public spectacle (Col 2:15). All the forces of moral and natural evil—imperial evil, religious evil, demonic evil—converge literally in an earthquake in one place, in one moment

98

in time (Matt 27:51). There, concentrated in the pain-wracked body of Jesus himself, with the virus of sin isolated in his own flesh (2 Cor 5:21), he takes on "our shame" in himself (Heb 12:2), and destroys its power through his own sacrificial death (1 Cor 15:55-56). Through the resurrection, ascension, and sending of the Spirit, every Christian becomes a microcosm of Jesus, a cell in the larger body. We become the anti-virus, spreading reconciliation in the space of flows throughout the whole system (2 Cor 5:18), until Jesus returns to bring the new creation in all its fullness (Matt 24:30, Rev 21–22).

In fresh expressions of church, as relationships are formed, some toxic theology about the human condition is encountered. Many people get hung up on "divine child abuse" theology: they hear that God the Father is punishing the hell out of his Son for our mistakes. Our Wesleyan understanding of restoration, the sacred worth and great value of every person, is refreshing to emerging generations. We emphasize the remarkable depth of God's love, to enter into the living hell we can inflict upon each other, to end the animal and grain sacrificial system and the need for violence once and for all. God descends into the deepest recesses of our human brokenness to show us who we really are, to heal our shame. This is indeed "good news" for most people.

The Fresh Expressions movement can be applied as a remix of the Wesleyan discipleship system. Once again, the "glad tidings of salvation" are being "proclaimed in the highways" and the fields. Now those fields and highways have taken the form of the nodes and flows of the network society.

People connect over hobbies, passions, and practices, across geographic barriers. Planting fresh expressions amid communities gathered around these practices involves an incarnational approach that ultimately transforms the practices themselves. The pioneers lead the group to begin intentionally exploring the Christian faith. This includes a mixture of both formal learning (intentional conversations) and social learning (simply sharing in the rhythms of life together). More mature believers may begin to form mentorships with younger apprentices, spending time outside the group, discipling them through the messy relational process.

Fresh Expressions is not about simply gathering in cool spaces to "play church." Very real disciples are being formed in these very real micro-churches, in much the same way as the early Methodist movement. At Wildwood, we've been experimenting with Wesley's model of societies, classes, and bands. We are in the process of identifying each one of our fresh expressions in one of those stages. Each of our fresh expressions is overseen by a pioneer, the "ordinary" Christian from among the "priest-hood of all believers."

So, for instance, at Tattoo Parlor Church and Paws of Praise (church in a dog park), God's prevenient grace is at work as we are regularly en-gaging not-yet-Christians and so called "nones" and "dones" and offering them Christ (society). In Burritos and Bibles (church in a Mexican restau-rant), Shear Love at Soul Salon, and Yoga Therapy Church, God's justify-ing grace is at work as people open up to Christianity, engage scripture, feel free to publicly pray, take communion for the first time, and share about "how goes it with their soul" (class). At Women, Wine, and the Word, a group of women gather in Francesco's Ristorante for the purposes of studying scripture, growing in sanctification, and brainstorming mis-sion opportunities in the community (band).[20]

While these contextual expressions may not be exacting illustrations of the early Wesleyan societies, we can see how they reflect a Methodism that's remerging powerfully through the Fresh Expressions movement.

In these gatherings, we've seen all kinds of beautiful grace moments unfold in people's lives along the journey as they are healed of their shame. When a young woman wept and said, "I slept with some guy Friday night and I don't even remember his name," the band of women enfolded her in love, and said things like, "That's not God's best for you, but we love you, we are with you." When's the last time something like that confession happened in a Sunday morning worship gathering? But isn't that the very

---

20. See https://freshexpressionsus.org/2018/03/05/history-repeating-discipleship/.

place in the universe where it should be happening? We've seen people go from praying publicly for the first time to leading their own fresh expression within a year's time. We've seen people convicted of their cursing, their smoking, their overeating, and be healed of their "isms."

I'm utterly convinced that fresh expressions, by creating places where folks can make the journey of grace and uncover the masterpiece beneath the mess, is making disciples in ways we have largely failed to do in the inherited church for decades.

Field Story—Beck

The 12 Steps/8 Principles of Celebrate Recovery (CR) mirror and are drawn from our Wesleyan *via salutis* "way of salvation."[21] Celebrate Recovery takes people through the continual movement toward Christian perfection, from "powerless and unmanageable" to "carrying the message and practicing the principles in all affairs" while seeking healing from all "hurts, habits, and hang ups."[22] This is the language we employ in our fresh expressions at Wildwood.

I've seen transformation lived out in one person I cherish and respect. Nicole Larrabee came to our church hurting and confused. I have journeyed beside her and watched this stunning transformative process of grace take place. Now, years later, she has responded to a call to pastoral ministry and serves as one of our pastors at Wildwood. God's amazing grace has seized and transformed her life.

God's prevenient grace reached out to Nicole through a CR program she attended to support a friend, until she realized that she was actually there for herself. As Nicole has realized on her journey of regeneration, we are all being healed continually one day at a time by the grace of God (Matt 6:34). Nicole has now responded by accepting her own call

---

21. Maddox rightly prefers "way" over "order." See *John Wesley's Practical Theology* (Nashville: Kingswood), 158.

22. John Baker, *Celebrate Recovery* (Grand Rapids, MI: Zondervan, 2012), 70.

to pastoral ministry and offering her life as a sacrifice. She has pioneered multiple fresh expressions, including a large worship gathering we call WildGlory (a multiethnic musical jam session that resembles a society meeting: prevenient grace), a micro-church in a nursing home (which resembles a class meeting: justifying grace), and a fresh expression in a coffee shop called Mascara Mondays for "women seeking to be sanctified and single" (a modern band meeting: sanctifying grace).

Nicole moved through these waves of grace, and now she has given her life to helping others move through them.

Missiography—Dangerous Prayers (Acevedo)

Before coming to Grace Church, I served as executive pastor at Christ Church, a thriving turnaround congregation in Fort Lauderdale under the visionary leadership of Dick Wills, now a retired United Methodist bishop. As a young pastor, that amazing congregation gave me exposure so some of the most innovative Christian ministries and leaders of that time.

One leader was O. S. Hawkins, then the senior minister of First Baptist Church in the heart of downtown Fort Lauderdale. O. S. led First Baptist in an amazing turnaround, and he taught me what I call a "dangerous prayer." He told me that this prayer sparked the turnaround of First Baptist Church, so I stored the prayer away for a time when I might need it as a leader. The prayer was simple. "Lord, send us the people nobody else wants." That's it. It's that simple.

So in 1996, I was sent by God and my bishop (in that order) to serve as the new lead pastor of Grace United Methodist Church in Cape Coral. I thought I was heading to Coral Gables near Miami. I had dreams of hanging out with Shaquille O'Neal and Madonna. You can imagine my shock when I looked at a map and discovered I was moving one hundred fifty miles on the other side of the state to Southwest Florida, home of beautiful manatees and many retired midwesterners.

In 1996, Grace Church was half full of beautiful people that seemingly had "lost their way." Very little transformational ministry within or outside of the church was happening. A huge mortgage on a sanctuary was hanging over our heads, and sadly on my first day "on the job" we had exactly $29.16 in the checking account.

But I did have that "dangerous prayer" (which is also a mission statement) in my back pocket. So naively and by faith, I began walking the buildings in great need of fresh paint and began earnestly praying, "Lord, send us the people nobody else wants." And little by little in those first few months and then in droves for the years following, God brought to us many hurting and broken people looking for hope and help in Jesus. Our teams began creating places for people to heal and many, many people were transformed.

As my tenth anniversary at Grace Church approached in 2006, I felt a nudge from the Holy Spirit to expand this "dangerous prayer." For whatever reason, my heart was captured by the reality of so many people feeling unnoticed in our community and world. They were the "Mr. Cellophane" from the hit Broadway show "Chicago" who sang: "Cellophane. Mister Cellophane, shoulda been my name. Mister Cellophane, 'cause you can look right through me, walk right by me and never know I'm there." So in 2006, we revised our prayer, "Lord, send to us the people nobody else wants or sees."

Then in 2011 while the entire globe was climbing out of the "great recession," the Holy Spirit began to nudge me again. "Add to the prayer." "But what, Lord?" "Say: 'Lord, send us *to* the people nobody else wants or sees." This transposition of the preposition *to* was a game changer for us. I didn't know it then, but it's really a fresh expression of church that honors both the inherited, attractional, "come to us" church and the fresh expressions, missional, "come to you" church. It is a prayer that releases all of the people of God to join Jesus in his movement. So, how about joining me in this "dangerous prayer?"

"Lord, send to us the people nobody else wants or sees. And Lord, send us to the people nobody else wants or sees."

Missional Field Kit
Mapping Milestones on
the Journey of Grace

With your team, discuss the journey of grace. Look at how John Wesley organized the societies, classes, and bands, corresponding with "waves of grace"—prevenient, justifying, and sanctifying.

Here are some questions to consider together:

1. How is the Holy Spirit "making disciples of Jesus Christ" in our church? How are we collaborating?

2. What is the "sin-bentness" pervading our community (for example, shame, guilt, racism, addiction, and so on)? How do we know this?

3. Where are we creating space or gatherings for people in the "prevenient grace" leg of their journey—those who may not be Christians yet?

4. Where are we creating space or gatherings for people in the "justifying grace" leg of their journey—those accepting Christ, and working out the implications for their lives?

5. Where are we creating space or gatherings for people in the "sanctifying grace" leg of their journey—those seeking to "love God and neighbor with all their heart, soul, mind, and body"?

6. How many people in our congregation are involved in ministry—leading, serving, and volunteering?

7. How many "pioneers" are actively seeking to form community with people outside the church?

You may find it helpful to draw out your responses on a whiteboard, to map out the milestones on the journey of grace.

Jesus and the New Pantheon

As stated previously, Wesleyan theology is "conjunctive theology," which often holds differing thoughts together in creative tension. For instance, as we have seen, Jesus is both "fully human" and "fully God." There are dimensions of Jesus's realm "already here" and "not yet." God is a "seeking" and "sending" God. We believe in "prevenient" and "justifying" and "sanctifying" grace. Wesley preached in "pulpits" and "fields." A God-shaped church is both "missional" and "attractional." And when interacting with persons of other religions, we believe in "openness and conviction."[1]

I meet weekly with a group of folks in church basements and classrooms from various religious beliefs (Buddhists, Muslims, Hindus, and more). While most are not Christians, they meet for the same reason many people meet on Sunday mornings—they yearn to be closer with God, they desire the fellowship of other human beings, and some just want to stay sober. I once wondered why these folks met so faithfully on the church property throughout the week, but wouldn't darken the door of a church on Sunday morning. I have always seen the church as a place

---

1. Theodore Runyon, *The New Creation: John Wesley's Theology Today* (Nashville: Abingdon Press, 1998), 215.

of hope and healing, but many others do not share my sentiments. In the case of the anonymous fellowship to which I belong, although these folks may not proclaim faith in Jesus Christ, the Holy Spirit is active and alive in them and empowering them to live a different kind of life—one free of drugs and alcohol.

Early Methodists emphasized a personal experience of God as a loving being who relentlessly seeks and desires to be in relationship with all (Luke 15). We urgently desire that all humanity come to know the God revealed in Jesus Christ. That desire drove John Wesley out to the fields, and that desire has driven Methodists into their communities ever since. We are sent with hearts aflame with God's love, to give our lives to God's grand search and recovery effort, *and* simultaneously in radical openness we are aware that God is working in the people already before we get there.

Particularly our understanding of prevenient grace—*the grace that goes before us*—is drawing all humanity into a relationship. This understanding should shape our interactions with people from other religions, as well as "nones and dones." Søren Kierkegaard said, "Christ is the Truth inasmuch as he is the way. [One] who does not follow the way also abandons the truth. We possess Christ's truth only by imitating him, not by speculating about him."[2] God the Son, as "the way," came to heal the brokenness of humanity, not just a single people group. Christ continually reaches out to the marginalized (Matt 15:21-28), those considered racially or religiously impure (John 4), and the religious other excluded from the community (Luke 7). God the Spirit continues to push those bounds and "go native" (Acts 2:8), operating in the world through all the diverse people God the Father has created (Acts 11:12). The very diversity of the peoples of the earth is a reflection of the diverse singularity of the Trinity (Gen 1:27).

This "conjunctive theology" put on flesh for me while working in Guatemala among indigenous religions. I went convicted to offer Christ. What I discovered was Christ had "gone native" before me. In the midst

---

2. Søren Kierkegaard, *Training in Christianity*, quoted in Michael Frost and Alan Hirsch, *ReJesus: A Wild Messiah for a Missional Church* (Peabody, MA: Hendrickson, 2009), 53.

of institutionalized poverty, I saw *agape* (love). My mind was opened to recognize that the Holy Spirit was already working. My heart was opened to the shamefulness of proclaiming a highly personalized, spiritualized, Western message of salvation with no contextual specificity.[3] I want all people to accept Christ, but whether they do or not—I must accept them. That experience shaped my missional mindset in the pioneering of fresh expressions.

Gil Rendle noted that the church was planted in an "aberrant time." This refers to a non-repeatable amalgamation of conditions to form a particular historical moment.[4] The twentieth-century conditions that enabled the thriving of a Christendom model for the church are no more. We are jungle people who must now learn to live in a desert. The ecosystem has changed, and our relationship with the environment is part of the challenge to live in a new world.

Following Christ's incarnational model, we must "go native," enter the world of the other, love them, and pursue the relational opportunities that naturally unfold. At the church I serve, more come to Christ in church parking lots and basements, tattoo parlors, restaurants, and dog parks, throughout the week than in the sanctuary. Fresh expressions are stocked ponds for "people fishing" (Matt 4:19). And so, with deep conviction *and* total openness, we must take Wesley's statement to heart: "Though we may not think alike, may we not all love alike?"[5]

Time for a Remix

In the United States, at least two generations have grown up in a rapidly secularizing and pluralistic culture. Today, emerging generations are

3. E. Tamez, *The Amnesty of Grace: Justification by Faith from a Latin American Perspective* (1993), 21.

4. Gilbert R. Rendle, *Quietly Courageous: Leading the Church in a Changing World* (Lanham, MD: Rowman & Littlefield, 2019), 21–23.

5. John Wesley, *The Standard Sermons in Modern English*, ed. K. C. Kinghorn (Nashville, 2002), 102.

growing up with a predominantly minimal experience of church. For a few more years, the majority in attendance at most congregations are "the builders," those born before 1946, who endured the Great Depression and World War II. The inevitable departure of these saints into the rest of God, and the convergence of other forces, was described by Lovett Weems as a "death tsunami," which statistically crested in 2018. This analogy can easily apply to churches across the theological and denominational spectrum.[6]

The era of "Blue Laws," those restrictions designed to ban Sunday activities to promote the observance of a day of Sabbath, is over. The age of Christendom, which was governed by white Christian Protestants, is past; the age of the new pantheon has come. The Roman pantheon described the constituency of all the gods collectively; it included the noteworthy gods of subjugated peoples. There are multiple similarities between ancient paganism and contemporary relativism.[7] The new US religious landscape is of the potluck variety. All religious paths are equally valid and meaningful, just take a sample of each if you like, and save room for dessert! This is called "personal religion" by sociologists. In the new pantheon for personal religion, all the "gods" share the same mythical space. Which "god" or combinations of "gods" one chooses is more a matter of personal preference than a matter of ultimate significance. Which "god" works best for you? Spirituality for personal religion is privatized and marketed to consumers like all other aspects of life.

In personal religion, each of the many "gods" has a devoted tribe. What Jesus called mammon, or money, is the true Zeus—king of the gods—in the theism of consumerist society. Len Sweet writes, "The market has become a god and consumption a religion.... The empire of goods has become the empire of our gods."[8]

---

6. Lovett H. Weems, *Focus: The Real Challenges That Face The United Methodist Church* (Nashville: Abingdon Press, 2011), 2.

7. David Goodhew, Andrew Roberts, and Michael Volland, *Fresh!: An Introduction to Fresh Expressions of Church and Pioneer Ministry* (London, UK: SCM Press, 2012), 4–5.

8. Leonard I. Sweet, *Me and We: God's New Social Gospel* (Nashville: Abingdon Press, 2014), 99–101.

Emerging generations hyper-connected by digital flows are rarely sold out to a single "tribe." They push against institutional iterations of religion that seem hypocritical and archaic. They also rarely commit to a single organization. As noted earlier, this doesn't mean they won't participate in an organization; it means they want to enjoy the freedom of participating in several organizations whose values and interests align with their own.

Therefore, one default spiritual mode in the United States is agnostic. Some educational systems train us to be skeptical and to apply critical thinking concerning every truth claim. Regrettably, some educated persons think their reason is superior, which can make them arrogant toward the other, unable to critique, for example, a scientific world view in tension with a-religious faith.

While there is a profound spiritual openness in our culture, one of the fastest growing tribes is the *none*—those who indicate no religious affiliation. While the language may be moving away from religiosity and toward all-inclusive spirituality, religion is very much alive in the United States. For example, consider a religious devotion to sports: the gladiatorial games of the new Rome. Consider "the largest religious revival you know nothing about." Heather Smith coined the term "Athletica" as she playfully, satirically but with compelling obviousness, noted how by every metric, youth sports leagues have all the major characteristics of a religion. There is liturgy, multiple weekly meetings, rituals, behavioral covenants, sacrifices, uniforms, worship gatherings, and membership fees. In fact, families demonstrate incredible devotion to sports in an unprecedented way. One could question if the American church in the twentieth century ever engaged and claimed people's whole lives this way.[9] On any given Sunday, many families welcome Lady Athletica to the US pantheon!

The New Testament emerged in a pantheistic environment. Paul's proclamation of the gospel and the early church spread in this type of culture. In the book of Acts we see faith communities quick on their feet

---

9.   Heather Smith, "Inside America's Largest Religious Revival You Know Nothing About," *The Federalist,* November 2017, http://thefederalist.com/2017/11/10/inside-americas-largest -religious-revival-know-nothing/, accessed November 2017.

and highly responsive. Christian theology and the structures of the church were taking shape as they emerged in the process of mission through engaging the contextual realities. For instance:

Acts 6:1-7. Leadership was applied and improvised from a missional imperative.

Acts 11:1-18. The Spirit guided the church to abolish long held convictions that divided people along racial and religious lines—to "make no distinction between them and us" (11:12).

Acts 15. The church "gathered" (Jerusalem, inherited) and "scattered" (Antioch, a fresh expression of church). They cooperated, conferenced, and made major adjustments for the sake of the greater mission (15:28-29).

Acts 16. Context determined Paul's missional approach. At Philippi, there were no synagogues, so Paul found "a place of prayer" down by the river. A fresh expression of church was born in Lydia's home.

Acts 17:1-9. The disciples disturbed the imperial peace, rather than cooperated with it, and engaged in non-violent subversion (17:7).

Acts 17:16-34. Paul adjusted to context. A true innovator, he used cultural phenomenon as a medium of proclamation (17:22-24).

Let's consider Paul's experience in Athens at the Areopagus:

While Paul was waiting for them in Athens, he was deeply distressed to see that the city was full of idols. (Acts 17:16 ESV)

First, Paul had the uncanny ability to pay attention to a context, to see both the fragmentation and the possibilities. Do we see our own contexts in this way? Listening, paying attention, looking for the sore spots in our community with soft eyes is crucial in healthy missional engagement. Next, he was "distressed," meaning his heart was troubled by the condition of the city. Do we care enough about our own zip code to be distressed over the fragmentation? Genuine care for our community, a healthy love for the people in it, is the starting point of every vital fresh expression of church.

Paul traveled to a third place, a space that served as the center of their curiosity:

> All Athenians as well as the foreigners who live in Athens used to spend their time doing nothing but talking about or listening to the newest thing. Paul stood up in the middle of the council on Mars Hill and said, "People of Athens, I see that you are very religious in every way." (Acts 17: 21-22)

Athens was the cradle of Greek civilization and a place that valued education. There were two major schools of thought—the Stoics and the Epicureans. In Paul's day, the Areopagus had become a forum for the exchange of free-flowing ideas between Epicureans, Stoics, and other philosophers. Paul was advantaged in having an extensive education among the Pharisees. He was highly competent in the skill of *translation*: the ability to build a bridge of meaning between culture and the gospel. Paul paid attention, analyzed culture, and started by affirming the life-giving tendencies already present in the culture: "I see that you are very religious in every way." He started by constructing the bridge of meaning on their side of the shore.

He continued in the Areopagus Address:

> As I was walking through town and carefully observing your objects of worship, I even found an altar with this inscription: "To an unknown God." What you worship as unknown, I now proclaim to you. (Acts 17: 22-23)

In his message, he used the inscriptions on their own temples as a medium for his proclamation. He did his homework and integrated what he had to say with their locality in a contextually appropriate way. He quoted their own poets and philosophers; he used their own soundtracks on the Billboard Hot 100 Chart and their own *New York Times* Best Sellers lists.

He respected the people enough to immerse himself in their context and thinking. He acknowledged what was good, beautiful, and true in their culture. He even nodded toward their pantheistic conceptions, but then unabashedly lifted the truth of Jesus.

In the network society, the web as a global integrated communication system is (on some nodes in social networks) the new Aeropagus. Manuel Castells notes that the culture of real virtuality

> weakens considerably the symbolic power of traditional senders external to the system, transmitting through historically encoded social habits: religion, morality, authority, traditional values, political ideology...unless they *recode* themselves in the new system, where the power becomes multiplied by the electronic materialization of the spiritually transmitted habits (italics mine).[10]

Paul and his missionary teams were *recoding* themselves, programming the truth of Jesus into the Greco-Roman system. John Wesley and the early Methodists recoded the Christian faith into the dawning industrial society (as well as the emerging European colonial expansion), in "plain words for plain people" by harnessing the emerging technologies. This is what fresh expressions pioneers are up to today.

In an age when the space of flows and the space of places coexist and interconnect, and a presence in the digital landscape makes a physical building unnecessary for the encounter, pioneers are harnessing social media and networking technologies to create Jesus communities in and among those larger networks. People are connecting and meeting in communal spaces in new relational arrangements that look like the church in Acts, "recoding" Christian truth into the system. We can be an incarnate presence on the digital frontier, harnessing these technologies that have become the means through which fresh expressions of church are organized, promoted, and sustained. By creating "disruptive innovation

---

10. Manuel Castells, *The Rise of the Network Society* (Oxford and Malden, MA: Blackwell, 2000), 406.

departments" in local churches, we can bypass the traditional ways that churches once solely relied upon to engage the community.

In social media flows, we connect with those outside typical church circles. Just as technology has become an extension of the human mind, so it is becoming an extension of the human communities of faith. Emerging generations who get their news through social media will also have their first encounters with churches through social media.

Most fresh expressions create free pages to describe basic info and location times that can be shared throughout an extensive relational network. Events can be created, friends invite friends. A relational cascade can stretch out far and wide across the digital landscape. People outside one person's relational network may be reached through another. Some fresh expressions use meetup.com or other similar platforms to create groups and invite new people. The hyper-connectivity that the internet provides can be harnessed to build actual communities in real first, second, and third places.

The inherited congregation may have the traditional centralized platform with websites and social media pages, like nodes and hubs within the network. But the fresh expressions serve as a decentralized "network" of relational transactions. Any person who can use social media can start a new fresh expression, organize a movement, or share a message. Wise churches will harness this capacity rather than attack it. While it challenges denominational systems, professional clergy, dedicated facilities, and traditional communication channels, if embraced or permitted, it could release the next remixed iteration of the church.

Churches have been largely focused on competing for the dwindling population of "already Christians" while blinded to the larger reality of the new pluralistic culture. Fresh expressions are about cultivating churches in the "fields" with this growing demographic of "nones and dones." It's about forming relationships with the spiritually open in the places where they do life. This is how Christianity spread like a virus through the Greco-Roman colonizing networks, and it is how the Evangelical Revival spread across the seas.

Field Story—Beck

"So, this is church? Man, this is F'n cool!" It's hard to forget the words of the young man who showed up for the first time that day. I'm abbreviating the word he said, due to original connotations, but I remember desiring so much that we would hear that adjective used to describe church more often: "F'n cool." When was the last time someone showed up to our Sunday morning traditional service and said that? What if we could create a church where not-yet-Christians would say that regularly?

One of the most controversial fresh expressions at Wildwood is Tattoo Parlor Church. We've received hate mail and been called everything from false prophets to a Satanic cult over this faith community. This is a full expression of the church, gathering in Fat Kat's Artistry in downtown Ocala. This experience features prayer, conversation around scripture, sharing tattoo stories, Holy Communion, and singing a couple of songs. And people get tattoos. Each person submits their art to our artists in advance, and we go back one by one into the bays as the community gathers in the front waiting area of the shop to worship Jesus. It's typical to see thirty to forty people packed into that space, sitting on the floor or wherever they can fit, to participate.

Tattooing is a prevalent practice in our culture. Nearly four in ten millennials (38 percent) are inked up, and over half of those have more than one tattoo. Gen Xers trail slightly behind with 32 percent sporting one or multiple tattoos.[11] Tattoo parlors are one of the busiest third places in some communities, particularly on the weekends. There is an entire culture built up around tattooing, piercing, and body modification. What are the chances that people deeply embedded in tattoo culture will show up to church on a Sunday morning? Very slim. For one, they are in tattoo parlors on Sunday. So, we have found a way to be church with them.

In that tattoo parlor, we've seen people very distant from the church enter a life-giving relationship with Jesus Christ. The seeking and sending

11. Paul Taylor, *The Next America: Boomers, Millennials, and the Looming Generational Showdown* (New York: Public Affairs, 2015), 58.

God is very much at work there. People randomly coming into the space have joined us. The artists, who were initially not Christian, have become Christian. Atheists who need a safe place to vent their frustration have shared. People with horns (literally, surgical implants) wearing Satan t-shirts have taken communion.[12] People have prayed out loud for the first time in their lives. Young folks have dumped out the shame and guilt they've been carrying. All of this is "normal" in these gatherings.

Some readers might be thinking, "But what about the tattoos? Doesn't the Bible say not to do that?" The passage that folks often refer to here is Leviticus 19:28, "You shall not make any gashes in your flesh for the dead or tattoo any marks upon you: I am the Lord" (NRSV). While there is a vast disconnect between the art of tattooing and the ancient practice of gashing and printing marks on one's flesh to lament the dead, a stronger argument for the practice of tattooing can be made more simply.

Read Leviticus 19, the whole chapter. Ask yourself these questions: Did you leave the edges of your field un-reaped for the gleaners? Did you plant two kinds of seed in your garden? Are you wearing clothing woven from two kinds of material? Was the fruit you ate today from a tree that had not been harvested until after five years? Did that cheeseburger or steak have any traces of blood in it? Did you trim your bangs anytime recently? Did you shave or trim the corners of your beard? (Yes, the idea is that all males should look like Hasidic Jews). Did you work a week recently without taking a day off? (By the way, you can sleep with your "female slave" if, of course, she's not pledged to another.) In other words, did you follow all six hundred thirteen commandments in the Torah? The answer is probably no, and yet we lift out this restriction about tattoos for dead loved ones and call those with tattoos "sinful."

I could make the case that God also has tattoos—"Look, on my palms I've inscribed you" (Isa 49:16)—or that in Jesus's triumphant return, he's wearing a robe dipped in blood, with blazing eyes, a sword in his mouth,

12. See Matt's interview at Tattoo Parlor Church on YouTube at https://youtu.be/t1qFVfDmTd4.

and tatt'd up, "He has a name written on his robe and on his thigh: King of kings and Lord of lords" (Rev 19:16). I am not suggesting that the Old Testament is an unreliable scriptural guide for faith and practice. This is a hyperbolic and playful reflection on how we pick and choose pieces of the Bible through the lens of our own contextualization. In fact, we often fall into dualism when we separate law and grace. The Israelites understood the Torah as instruction about a way of life, rather than as the Law—an understanding that emerged among Roman interpreters of Pharisaic Judaism. So, we need to be careful about celebrating that the "good news" means that we are no longer "bound by the law." And yet it remains entirely true that we live by grace through faith in Jesus Christ: "Sin will have no power over you, because you aren't under Law but under grace" (Rom 6:14).

I did not expect to be so deeply incarnate within tattoo culture. When I was introduced to Brian, the shop owner, our "peace maker," I did not imagine seven years later we would still be church there. It wasn't until I started to see the incredible things God was up to in the space that I was compelled to really put some skin in the game. Pun intended. The prevenient grace of God is at work. Yes, even in the tattoo parlor, God is already at work before we get there—wooing, transforming, speaking, and healing.

Tattooing is an art form. Wesley held that there were two sacraments: baptism and communion, and that these were "means of the grace." There are other means that are not "sacramental" in this sense, for instance: prayer, love, studying scripture, fasting, and so on. Wesleyans see the means of grace as an outward expression of an inner transformation. For some, tattoos can be a means of grace. Every tattoo tells a story, such as the friend who got crosses tattooed over the scars on her wrists where she tried to commit suicide. Or the young adult who got *imago Dei* in her deceased mother's handwriting written in rainbow ink to remind her she is made in the image of God. Approximately fifty members of Tattoo Parlor Church have the cross and flames proudly inscribed in their flesh, because they found true life in The United Methodist Church that gathers in a tattoo parlor.

These are not random symbols but a new form of sacred iconography. Cathedrals told the story of Jesus to the illiterate in their stained-glass windows. We tell the story of Jesus to the biblically illiterate on our arms, legs, and feet, inscribed in our temples of flesh. These spiritual symbols are conversation starters about our faith. They give us a way to talk about Jesus to others. Many times, someone has asked about my tattoos, opening the door for me to tell my story with Jesus. This is not exactly a new sign of grace. Wassim Razzouk is one of the most renowned tattoo artists in the world. In Jerusalem, his family has been inking Christian pilgrims with sacred symbols for over five hundred years.[13]

In a network society, this is what I mean by gathering in communities of practice. Over time, the practices themselves are transfigured to point to the Lordship of Jesus.

Missiography—From the Synagogue to the Lecture Hall (Acevedo)

On Monday, October, 24, 2015, during my daily time of Bible reading, reflecting, and journaling, I read a passage in Acts and wrote:

> Then Paul went to the synagogue and preached boldly for the next three months, arguing persuasively about the kingdom of God. But some became stubborn, rejecting his message and publicly speaking against the Way. So Paul left the synagogue and took the believers with him. Then he held daily discussions at the lecture hall of Tyrannus. (Acts 19:8-9 NLT)
>
> Paul is in Ephesus. When he arrived, he found twelve believers in Jesus who had never heard of the Holy Spirit. Paul explained who the Holy Spirit is and then prayed for them to experience the baptism in the Spirit. With his core team established, Paul, a generative team leader, began his typical strategy that had worked for him in other places. He began teaching in the local synagogue. His approach was

---

13. See https://www.christiantoday.com/article/tattoo-artist-upholds-centuries-old-tradition-of-marking-pilgrims-during-their-visit-to-holy-land/128544.htm.

to engage Jewish believers in the gospel. As Jesus was a Jew, there was a commonality between his message and their experience. Openness to the gospel by Jews was evident in Jerusalem and other places. This was a fruitful strategy that had worked and was working. Instead of welcome in the Ephesians synagogue, Paul experienced significant pushback. Instead of "pushing this rock up a hill," Paul abandoned his strategy after three months while staying true to his grander mission of making disciples in every place. He moved to a new "third place" and began a "fresh expression" of Christianity. He began holding "daily discussions" in a lecture hall, not "preaching" in a synagogue. A new place with new unreached people demanded a new strategy.

Paul demonstrates what may be the future of the mission of Jesus in America. "Preaching in the synagogue" has its place. The "inherited church" is still working in many places. Investing energy in this strategy is essential. But emerging and expanding clusters of unreached people are the "nones and dones." The inherited church is too weak in capacity and motivation to reach these clusters. So we are faithful to the gospel while we allocate resources in a "blended ecology" of inherited church and fresh expressions.

For example, I prayed at a Habitat for Humanity home blessing. The new house is less than a mile from our Cape Coral campus. There was such openness to God in that beautiful new home. But not so evident was an openness to the inherited church. I invited, but I'm not sure what the outcome will be. On the home turf, the nature of the conversation changes. Intentionally multiplying these kinds of interactions will be our challenge at any church. Having spaces, places, and people in all kinds of new and innovative "third places" will be our challenge if we are faithful to Paul's example.

> Lord, help us not be so married to our strategies that we miss new Spirit-inspired opportunities. Give us the wisdom of Paul to sense when a new strategy needs to emerge for the spreading of the gospel. Blow a fresh wind of the Spirit across our church God. Give your old men and old women new dreams. Give your young men and young women new visions. Help us catch up to what you are doing in the world. Amen.

Four years after writing this, God indeed is raising up men and women, young and old, to join Jesus in these new and innovative "third spaces." From community centers to pizza parlors, from mountain bike courses to parks, the Holy Spirit is using new strategies to connect with new people.

Missional Field Kit
Recoding Exercises—Finding Good
News in the Culture

This is an exercise in interpreting culture. Gather your fresh expressions team together and play one or each of the following YouTube clips. Simply watch, and then ask yourself these three questions:

1. What touched you about this clip?

2. Where did you see the gospel?

3. How would you use this piece as a medium to tell someone about God?

- Lion King: https://youtu.be/yGQnGQzlAm
- "This Is Me": https://youtu.be/XLFEvHWD_NE
- Ikea Commercial: "Start Something New" https://youtu.be /lQwrpmUmVeo

Perhaps you have another movie clip, song, commercial, or cultural piece that would be more appropriate for your context. The main idea here is to find the "good news" in the culture and how to use it as a bridge to the truth of Jesus.

A God of *Withness* in a World of Hurt

The Methodist revival was formed in the crucible of a society plagued with suffering and evil. Len Sweet writes, "John Wesley led the Wesleyan revival at a time when his culture was in the midst of one of the worst crime waves in English history."[1] The movement took place in a time of massive inequality and exploitation. The snares of drink, gambling, prostitution, degrading sports, and indifference to Christianity were the norm.

> Fifty-five percent of children died before age five. There was an alehouse for every twenty households. London was the sex capital of the world, like Amsterdam and Bangkok today. Throughout the eighteenth century, London had more prostitutes per capita than any other European city.[2]

In the underbelly of this immense suffering and evil, the people called Methodists became an incarnational presence. Wesley intentionally chose the disreputable spots, the seedy places of ill repute, earning

---

1. Leonard I. Sweet, *Me and We: God's New Social Gospel* (Nashville: Abingdon Press, 2014), 33.

2. Leonard I. Sweet, *The Greatest Story Never Told: Revive Us Again* (Nashville: Abingdon Press, 2012), 86.

the reputation as the "pastor of the mob." He wrote, "I bear the rich and love the poor, therefore I spend almost all of my time with them."[3] Wesley considered it his calling to offer a loving "withness" in the sore spots of English society; he "worked against electoral corruption; structured systematic distribution of food, medicine, clothing, loans, and money; and organized temporary employment for the destitute."[4] Methodist gatherings were a great equalizer, where people of all walks of life came together as one.

When humanity rebelled against God, the mutability of creation was revealed, and sin, death, and evil entered the equation. A loving God immediately sought out beloved creation with the missional call, "Where are you?" (Gen 3:9). This is the cosmic narrative in which humanity has participated ever since. Furthermore, free will is not something unique to humanity; it characterizes all creatures and things, revealing an element of randomness. Rather than God micromanaging creation in a deterministic fashion, God is shaping a world with divine purposes and possibilities as humans emerge through the process of becoming.[5] Sin is not simply rebellion against God but against creation. While epic goodness, beauty, and truth is baked into the "very good" creation, the universe as we currently know it is corrupted; not only does humanity need redemption, so does creation itself (Rom 8:22). Death, disease, and natural disasters (natural evil), as well as human evil flourishing in individuals, institutions, and systems (moral evil) are obvious features of our current sin-broken cosmos.

The historic position of Methodists in this scenario is *withness*, which means faithful presence *with* the sufferer. Further, we believe in a God of withness in a world of hurt.

---

3. Wesley, *Letters*, Vol. IV, p. 266. To Ann Foard, 29 September, 1764.

4. Sweet, *Me and We*, 33.

5. Tyron Inbody, *The Faith of the Christian Church: An Introduction to Theology* (Grand Rapids, MI: Eerdmans, 2005), 155–57.

Time for a Remix

"If God is good, how can there be so much suffering and evil in the world?" This is one of the most consistent and profound questions "nones and dones" wrestle with in our fresh expressions of church.

While I don't have a sufficient explanation for why there is suffering and evil in the world, Methodists claim to experience God's sustaining presence in the midst of it. God somehow uses it, and more particularly as the church... we *are* sometimes God's answer to it. We partner with God to overcome the evil and suffering. Although I don't believe God causes suffering or evil to exist, they undeniably are pervasive forces throughout my life. As we learn to pioneer fresh expressions, we understand that there are questions and tragedies for which no answer will suffice, and yet we persist in the mystery.

I grew up in a world of strange dualisms: of light *and* dark, of mean streets *and* soft sanctuary pews, of ruthless victimizers *and* selfless saints, of deep hunger pains *and* extravagant potluck spreads. It was a very *good* world, but plagued with suffering and evil. I was born addicted, abandoned at birth, and my biological father unknown. My mother, a beautiful child of God, afflicted with addiction, fell into a life of prostitution. When I was ten years old, my grandfather (that is, my adopted father) died of cancer. My grandmother, who introduced me to church, died in my arms several years later.

Like the early Methodists, the people of St. Mark's UMC entered that dark journey and loved me within it. Even so, I squandered my early life with alcohol and dissolute living. I know well the path of suffering and evil. I walked it. I have felt the weight of institutional evil in an unjust economic machine that systematically oppresses some while a small minority profit from their suffering. I have felt the crushing desperation of poverty and abandonment. Ultimately, on the floor of a jailhouse while going through withdrawal, I cried out to Jesus in desperation. Christ came to me in a powerfully personal way that changed my life forever. I returned to the spiritual orphanage of my childhood, where a recovering alcoholic pastor nurtured me as a son.

More than a decade of continuous sobriety from all substances, years of therapy, spiritual direction, and mentorship has passed. I cannot forget those dark days, nor do I want to. Through that adversity God has forged me as a servant. Now I realize it's not my righteousness that God uses most powerfully; it's my brokenness. God does not cause suffering, but God has used mine to bring healing to others.

As an ordained pastor, I continuously encounter evil and the suffering that often results. I was present at the birth of a child, baptized her, then only weeks later conducted her memorial service when she died from blunt-force trauma. I have counseled victims of abuse, heard the confessions of abusers, and spent countless hours in the intensive-care units of hospitals and the final stop in hospice. I prayed for a young woman in her twenties as she died in the presence of her panic-stricken family. I watched cancer devastate faithful saints who loved God. I held the hand of a woman infected with AIDS in the final moments of her life as she called out for Jesus. I prayed over bewildered response teams deployed in the wake of devastating natural disasters, such as the hurricanes that ravage our state, or the earthquake in Haiti. Honestly, in some of those situations I felt confused, inadequate, and speechless. I have also heard such well-meaning but misguided statements as, "Well, I guess God needed an angel" or "Nothing happens by mistake." Unwittingly, those who make such statements are contributing to an image of a tyrannical, micromanager God demanding blood and causing suffering.

So when bringing fresh expressions of ministry to the "nones and dones," two aspects of God are held in creative tension: a temporal one, which is historical, relating, growing, and living, and one which is invulnerable, immutable.[6] God's triune power is demonstrated through a creating and transforming power, not through unilateral omnipotence. God's omnipotent power revealed in Jesus Christ is the power of withness and

6. Burton Cooper, *Why, God?* (Atlanta: John Knox, 1988), 80–90.

cruciform love, transforming death into rebirth, and making old creation "new creation."[7]

The Old Testament reveals the vulnerability and suffering of God, which are fully realized in the cross of Jesus. The cross breaks our old monarchial image of God and provides us with a new image, a crucified God who redeems us not by coercive power but by suffering *with us* in our suffering. David Hart warns against abstract answers in the midst of suffering.[8] Indeed, any level of "explanation" is not always comforting at the bedside of the sufferer.

In this world of darkness and light, I have seen the powerful way God's grace works among fallen realities. The church embodies "in its fallible, ambiguous way the transforming, healing power of Christ in the world."[9] The same church that plucked me from the darkness of my childhood is God's incarnate answer to suffering, a caring expression of Christ's redemptive power. We sing the love story of the cross.

Our response is not one of simple explanation but of *withness*. We point to a place where sin is overcome, for Christ suffered the vilest form of evil, yet defeated death, and will return to fully do away with sin and suffering (Rev 21). We wait *with* the suffering, as the caring presence listening with hope, manifesting God's compassion and tears (liquid prayers) to extend the strength of divine presence. We as the church proclaim that God's unconquerable love (Rom 8:31-39) and triune omnipotence will bring all things into renewal and perfection (Rev 21:5). This is the historic legacy of the people called Methodists. Fresh Expressions is providing us a way to be the hands and feet of Jesus in a hurting world. Not by simply waiting back in our pristine buildings, but by joining our "other" in their suffering, where they live. We can link with God as we offer loving withness in a world of hurt.

7. Inbody, *The Faith of the Christian Church*, 155–57.

8. David B. Hart, *The Doors of the Sea: Where Was God in the Tsunami?* (Grand Rapids, MI: Eerdmans, 2005), 99–100.

9. Cooper, *Why, God?* 15.

Field Story—Beck

One place we can see this theology lived out in a real way today, is in Seattle, Washington. This is the birthplace of the Dinner Church Collective that's now sweeping across the United States. Verlon and Melodee Fosner were fully immersed in the world of hurt in their community, trying to find a way to be a witness. In one of the most post-Christian places in the United States, they use the terminology of "sore neighborhoods." Verlon advocates a return to Jesus's "search and rescue" mission for the church and that we need to adopt a neighborhood theology. He points out that most churches have lost a meaningful connection with their contexts. In the attractional only model, there is little regard to the actual makeup of the neighborhoods where congregations are situated. If we can return to a theology of the neighborhood, churches exist to know and serve the greatest needs of their immediate neighbors.[10]

The Dinner Church Collective, under the larger umbrella of the Fresh Expressions movement, is plugging into two primary felt needs: hunger and isolation. These micro-churches are founded on a theology of the table, meaning church happens when people sit down to break bread together. Many dinner churches take place in sore communities, where there exist significant populations of the marginalized and lonely. If we take seriously the emerging economic reality of a hollowing of the middle, we can see that many churches are still targeting a middle class that largely no longer exists. Many American families visit food banks and live below the poverty line.

Last year, in partnership with Fresh Expressions US and the Fosners, we rolled out a Dinner Church initiative in the Florida Conference. Now approximately thirty dinner churches exist in sore neighborhoods spread through the state. In some cases, the inherited congregations have a dozen or so people in worship on Sunday mornings, but over fifty people gathering in a dinner church one evening throughout the week. Quickly, the

---

10. Verlon Fosner, *Dinner Church: Building Bridges by Breaking Bread* (Franklin, TN: Seedbed, 2017), 107–8.

attendance of these fresh expressions centered on a communal meal is outpacing the existing congregation. However, many people are also matriculating back to the Sunday morning services.

These churches are finding a way to be a loving *withness* in a world of hurt.

Missiography—My Three Conversions (Acevedo)

Three conversions have shaped my life. I do not know the exact date, but sometime in the middle of January in 1978, I became a follower of Jesus. This was my first conversion. A parachurch ministry, Campus Crusade for Christ, worked at my high school in Orlando, Florida. The Area Director poured himself into our school and lovingly pursued a genuine relationship with me. He embodied the gospel to this wandering and wondering, drug-and-alcohol-dependent senior. The night when I prayed and asked Jesus into my life, we were meeting at my home. My decision to follow Jesus was far from emotional. There were no tears or shouts. My "sinner's prayer" was more like a bet. "Lord, my friend John says you can give my life purpose and meaning. And if you can, I'll follow you." The One who had been pursuing me my entire life had "some" of my attention. And that was enough. My journey with Jesus began that night.

My second conversion happened about fifteen years later. By then, I was a married man with two children and an ordained United Methodist pastor serving in the Florida Conference at Christ Church in Fort Lauderdale. I would describe my second conversion as a conversion to embrace the Body and Bride of Christ, the church. Like many of my generation, I was at best institutionally suspicious. I thought of the church, especially the local church, in a utilitarian way. Church helped me "do my ministry."

But somewhere in the early 1990s two things happened. First, I began to experience a congregation making a significant difference in a community. Christ Church was doing innovative ministry among the poor and homeless in Broward County. We had pioneered a ministry to people with addictions that pushed back the walls of darkness in people's lives and in our community. This glimpse of a church following the biblical teaching of ministry with the poor endeared me to the Body of Christ.

In this setting, I began to read the New Testament differently. Classic texts about the purpose of the church, such as 1 Corinthians 12–14, exposed me to a new picture of a life-transforming local fellowship made up of women and men, filled with God's Spirit, and engaged in ministry that transformed communities and the world. The Bride of Christ was becoming for me the bright, holy, and radiant people of God, reconciled to God through Jesus and filled with the power of the Holy Spirit. I *fell in love* with the church.

My third conversion began in 2006. I had been at Grace Church for ten years and Wes Olds, my spiritual son, had joined our team as one of our pastors. He quickly diagnosed that I was stricken with a terminal case of "heroic, solo leader." At the time, everyone on staff, more than forty, reported to me. Almost all decisions came to my desk. Now this was not so much because I was a control freak, though many would disagree with me, but because as the church grew over a decade, we got comfortable letting me make all the decisions. The church was growing. It wasn't broken. Don't break it.

But the nagging secret is that this kind of management isn't sustainable. I was worn thin. Exhausted. The work I was doing for God was destroying the work of God in me. Wes kindly confronted my "heroic, solo" leadership style and offered me a new way: the way of the generative team leader. So, since then my church and I have taken a journey of developing healthy and holy teams that cultivate and create transformational environments and fruitful disciple-making processes. Not only have we gotten better at making disciples, but the weight of ministry is now owned and shared by ministry partners who passionately follow Jesus, love the church, and discover, develop and deploy spiritual leaders to join Jesus in his mission.

Missional Field Kit:
Searching for Sore Spots

What is sore in this community?

Following Paul's approach in Athens, conduct a "prayer walk" in your community with your team.[11] Perhaps use the people-map you created earlier. Plan a day for people to gather at your designated headquarters. Organize people in teams. Have others in the congregation cover you in prayer. Look for the "sore spots" in your community. Where do you see "hurt?" Ask yourselves, "God, what is breaking your heart in this community?" Do you have the boldness to pray, "Break our hearts for the things that break your heart?"

The key is to keep it simple. Focus on three basic practices: pray, observe, and encounter.

> **Prayer:** Have a conversation with God as you walk around together. Sensitize yourselves to the stirrings of the Holy Spirit: pray for specific homes, businesses, or schools. Pray over the streets, pray over the buildings, pray over the people.

> **Observation:** Pay attention to the context. This is simply a form of listening. How many people do you notice in the space? What are they doing? What are the conditions of the neighborhoods where you are? What kinds of isolation do you see? What kinds of practices are people participating in? Are people engaging each other in certain ways? How are they dressed? What ways do you see the Holy Spirit at work? What is God up to here?

> **Encounter:** This is not about a Romans road, sinner's prayer, or any of that other business. Nor is it about holding up "Jesus Saves" signs or blowing on bull horns. When God brings someone into your path, and the Spirit nudges toward encounter, start with, "Hello. What's your name? How are you doing today?"

---

11. For in-depth guidance about prayer walks, see Sue Nilson Kibbey, *Ultimate Reliance: Breakthrough Prayer Practices for Leaders* (Nashville: Abingdon Press, 2019).

Have your team gather together to share observations. Have someone in the group write down the details. Perhaps use a white board so you can visualize it together. Agree to pray over these observations together until you meet again. You may rediscover with the Wesley brothers that sore spots are the perfect places to cultivate fresh expressions of church.

O Give Me That Book!

I want to know one thing, the way to heaven, how to land safe on that happy shore. God has condescended to teach the way. For this very end God came down from heaven. God has written it down in a book. O give me that book! At any price, give me that book of God! I have it. Here is knowledge enough for me. Let me be homo unius libri.[1]

—John Wesley

Among the means of grace, which he drew from ancient Christian sources, Wesley encouraged Methodists to "search the scriptures," including daily engagement with the Old and New Testaments. He suggested that itinerant preachers "Fix some part of every day for private exercises.... Whether you like it or no, read and pray daily."[2] For Methodists, scriptural engagement and spiritual reading is the source of ongoing spiritual development.

Wesley said, "the substance of the entire Bible is summed up in two plain words: faith and salvation."[3] The Bible reveals God, enables us to develop faith, leads us to salvation (Rom 10:17), and calls us to be transformed into the character of God. "Through this faithful reading of

---

1. John Wesley, *Sermons on Several Occasions*, Preface, 1.5.

2. Steve Harper, *Devotional Life in the Wesleyan Tradition* (Nashville: Upper Room Books, 1995), 21.

3. John Wesley, *The Standard Sermons in Modern English,* ed. K. C. Kinghorn, (Nashville, 2002), Vol. 3, 187.

scripture, we may come to know the truth of the biblical message in its bearing on our own lives and the life of the world. Thus, the Bible serves both as a source of our faith and as the basic criterion by which the truth and fidelity of any interpretation of faith is measured."[4]

However, Wesley also instructed his Methodist preachers, "Spend all the morning, or at least five hours in twenty-four, in reading the *most useful* books, and that regularly and constantly."[5] He lifted up both the importance of continuous engagement with the scriptures, *and* the importance of reading widely to gain all manner of understanding. It is through this study that Methodists were able to cultivate contextual intelligence. They thrived by not only knowing the scriptures but by knowing the culture and knowing what to do. Engaging thinkers across the spectrum informed how they communicated the gospel. They learned to build bridges of meaning and translate that biblical practice to the wider culture in relevant ways.

As Scott Jones states, "Scripture alone.... Yet, never alone."[6] Followers in the Wesleyan way, and speaking specifically of my denomination (The United Methodist Church) do not wave a *sola Scriptura* banner. "Wesley believed that the living core of the Christian faith was revealed in Scripture, illumined by tradition, vivified in personal experience, and confirmed by reason."[7] While it did not originate with Wesley, this interdependent fourfold matrix, now identified as the "quadrilateral," is a powerful tool for Methodists to employ in our theological task to "reflect upon God's gracious action in our lives."[8] Let's briefly examine each of its elements.

Regarding tradition, the United Methodist *Book of Discipline* states, "Christianity does not leap from New Testament times to the present as

---

4. *The United Methodist Book of Discipline, 2012,* ¶104, 78.

5. Iain H. Murray, *Wesley and the Men Who* Followed (Edinburg: The Banner of Truth Trust, 2003), 89–90 (emphasis original).

6. Scott Jones, *United Methodist Doctrine: The Extreme Center* (Nashville: Abingdon Press, 2002), 136.

7. *The Book of Discipline, 2012,* ¶104, p. 77.

8. *The Book of Discipline, 2012,* ¶104, p. 74.

though nothing were to be learned from that great cloud of witnesses in between."[9] Christians always have been grappling with how to live out the gospel in a wide array of contexts. We draw from that depth of tradition by reaching back to the primitive church, including early creeds such as the Apostles' and Nicene-Constantinopolitan, various church councils, journeys of Christian pilgrims, and writings of Christian thinkers (Heb 12:1-2). This diverse witness has been preserved over the centuries. It contains the great triumphs and epic failures of our tradition, both from which we can learn.[10]

Our Christian experience also serves as a resource. Christian experience is "the personal appropriation of God's forgiving and empowering grace."[11] This highlights the necessary intersection of the Bible and our experience because "Our experience interacts with Scripture. We read Scripture in light of the conditions and events that help shape who we are, and we interpret our experience in terms of Scripture."[12] Thus, while we read scripture through the lens of our own formation, the Bible interprets our life.

God also gave us wonderful brains. Our ability to reason is a gift from God (Luke 14:28). By reason, we hear and interpret the scripture, wrestle with its truth, and thoughtfully apply it to our lives. Reason, unfortunately, is marred by sin, and is best used in community with others.[13]

One precious gift that Wesley has left us is a particular interpretive tool for the study of scripture: reading the whole of the Bible through the life, death, and resurrection of Jesus Christ. This tool has been called the "analogy of faith," "analogy of Christ," or a "Jesus hermeneutic" (a method of interpretation). Paul Chilcote wrote, "This simply means that the Christian should read Scripture through the eyes of Christ or through

---

9. *The Book of Discipline, 2012,* ¶105, p. 83.

10. Jones, *United Methodist Doctrine,* 138–39.

11. *The Book of Discipline, 2012,* ¶105, p. 81.

12. *The Book of Discipline, 2012,* ¶105, p. 85.

13. Jones, *United Methodist Doctrine,* 140.

the interpretive lens of the way of salvation. Jesus and the way of salvation through him become the measure of all things in terms of the meaning of the Bible."[14]

John Wesley made the Bible accessible to the masses, "plain words for plain people" and that enabled the movement to flourish. Proclaiming and embodying the scriptures in the fields was how he made the truth available to those marginalized masses outside the reach of the church. Wood notes historical writings that indicate preaching in England before the revival had declined to an intolerable dullness; many sermons had become merely "moral essays."[15] In contrast, John Wesley preached spontaneously "from the heart," and nearly every sermon was an invitation to respond practically to God's grace in the real world. He did not prepare manuscripts to be read in the fields. Many of the published sermons we have were never preached. They were "sermonic essays" that functioned as theological treatises.[16] Wesley, the scholar, adapted his methods for "spreading scriptural holiness" to fit the context.

Time for a Remix

In a post-Christendom age, coping with toxic Christian ideologies such as nationalism, fundamentalism, and dispensationalism,[17] many people become "nones and dones," indeed even atheists, through reading the Bible. One of the primary roles of a pioneer in fresh expressions is to encounter people beyond the reach of the institutional church. The challenge is faithfully to interpret and recode the Bible in a way that people can understand and so that they can reorient their lives around its guidance

14. Paul W. Chilcote, *John and Charles Wesley: Selections from Their Writings and Hymns* (Woodstock, VT: SkyLight Paths Publications, 2011), 202.

15. Arthur S. Wood, *The Burning Heart: John Wesley, Evangelist* (Minneapolis: Bethany Fellowship, 1978), 284–85.

16. Chilcote, *John and Charles Wesley*, 13.

17. See Paul W. Chilcote, *Active Faith: Resisting Four Dangerous Ideologies with the Wesleyan Way* (Nashville: Abingdon Press, 2019).

for faith and practice. A particularly exciting and challenging aspect of preaching and teaching the Bible in fresh expressions is the prophet-poet's "shattering, evocative speech that breaks fixed conclusions and presses us always toward new, dangerous, imaginative possibilities...this artistic speech voiced in the prophetic construal of the Bible is the primary thrust of the church and its preaching."[18] The Bible, when taught authentically, presents a counter-truth that shatters our reality. Furthermore, the process of discipleship, which comes from deep engagement with the Bible, involves learning to bend our lives to the instruction from scripture. Eugene Peterson wrote, "Christian spirituality is, in its entirety, rooted in and shaped by the scriptural text.... We are formed by the Holy Spirit in accordance with the text of Holy Scripture."[19]

However, in fresh expressions of church, scriptural engagement takes on many non-traditional contextually appropriate forms. Primarily, "sermons" are less about a single conductor leading an orchestra from the platform and more like the shared experience of an improvised jazz band. Rather than the "professional minister" teaching us what the Bible means, the sermon takes a communal form. We read a couple of verses, reflect upon what we've read, ask questions, and have a conversation. The community creates a sermonic experience together. Everyone has an opportunity to contribute. The people shape where the "sermon" goes. Fresh expressions are not the place for written manuscripts, and in many cases not even a structured teaching plan. Studying the text in advance, knowing it deeply, being prepared to go where the people lead, are the skills required of pioneers.

Burritos and Bibles, mentioned earlier, is the fresh expression that meets at Moe's Southwest Grill, where we study the scripture inductively and conclude with Holy Communion. This gathering aggregates folks from a variety of perspectives across the theological spectrum. We began

18. Walter Brueggemann, *Finally Comes the Poet* (Minneapolis: Fortress, 1989), 6–8.

19. Eugene Peterson, *Eat This Book: A Conversation in the Art of Spiritual Reading* (Grand Rapids, MI: Eerdmans, 2006), 15.

with four people and now fill the restaurant. For some who are not ready to participate in traditional "church" but willing to have a burrito, all-you-can-eat chips and salsa, and seek to better understand the Bible—this is their church. I love exploring together and watching how the Spirit often enlightens us through communal study.

Some of our fresh-expression pioneers lean more Calvinist in theology than Wesleyan. Some have no theological orientation at all. We try to encourage theological unity but not theological uniformity. We love the same Lord and often share our different perspectives. This brings us all to fuller understanding (Prov 27:17). However, while we may mostly agree that the biblical authors wrote under the inspiration of the Holy Spirit (2 Tim 3:16-17), we have some distinctions on exactly how the Bible is God's Word or contains God's word, that is, how the Bible is true.

I believe God inspired the authors of the scriptures, and that God worked through the process of editing, compiling, and canonization (which means establishing the books that are authorized for faith and practice). God continues to work in us now as we read. When I prepare, first I pray for the Spirit to illuminate my understanding of the text. However, I struggle with a literal interpretation of the Bible as "infallible and inerrant." I find these to be claims the Bible doesn't actually make for itself.

Here I appropriate John Wesley's "analogy of faith" or the "Jesus hermeneutic" mentioned above. Jesus understood Scripture as *authoritative*. He quoted Hebrew Bible texts often and claimed that his mission was to "fulfill" them (Matt 5:17). Yet his fulfillment, in some cases, is quite radical. This is made clear by his confrontations with the Pharisees (compare Deut 24:1 with Mark 10:2-9) and the "fulfillment" teachings: "you've heard it said . . . but I say." Jesus expands "eye for an eye" *to* "turn the other cheek," and "hate your enemies" *to* "love your enemies and pray for them" (Matt 5:17-48).

Further, Jesus himself directly reframes sections in the book of Leviticus that speak of "clean versus unclean" sins that require the death

136

penalty, and the seemingly crude restrictions concerning those with birth defects, people who are deformed, or the commandment that menstruating women are not allowed in community worship.[20] Also, even among the various accounts of the resurrection, the most profound moment in history, there are inconsistencies. Hence, I see Jesus as "the lens and filter of the *definitive* and *unmitigated* word of God" through which all of the Old and New Testaments should be read and understood.[21]

Thus, the authority of scripture is not based simply around a grouping of rules we must follow. This authority legitimates our mission. Authority authorizes our freedom to act within boundaries. From Genesis to Revelation, that mission starts with "Where are you?" and finds fulfillment in Christ—God eternally *with us*. The whole Bible points to Jesus Christ.

In confessing the scriptures together as the church, we become that Christ-centered community of which it speaks. "As we open our minds and hearts to the word of God through the words of human beings inspired by the Holy Spirit, faith is born and nourished."[22] We have continuity with the apostles and Israel. The Bible, as the primary source of authority, sufficient and revealing "the word of God," brings us into an encounter with the "living Word" (John 1:1,14), God incarnate in the person of Jesus Christ. As United Methodists, "We share with many Christian communities a recognition of the authority of Scripture in matters of faith, the confession that our justification as sinners is by grace through faith, and the sober realization that the church is in need of continual reformation and renewal."[23] Thus, "Through Scripture the living Christ meets us in

---

20. Will Willimon states "one encounters inconsistencies and contradictions, to say nothing of downright bad ideas in the Bible" (*This We Believe: The Core of Wesleyan Faith and Practice* [Nashville: Abingdon Press, 2010], 78).

21. Adam Hamilton, *Making Sense of the Bible: Rediscovering the Power of Scripture Today* (New York: HarperOne, 2014), 164–66; 175.

22. *The Book of Discipline, 2012,* ¶104, p. 78.

23. *The Book of Discipline, 2012,* ¶101, p. 44.

the experience of redeeming grace. We are convinced that Jesus Christ is the living Word of God in our midst whom we trust in life and death."[24]

The message it contains is true, as is the God it reveals. Hence, the Bible is true in a way that nothing else can be, because it introduces us to the one who is "the way, the *truth*, and the life" (John 14:6, emphasis mine). The centerpiece of pioneer ministry is its innovative proclamation in contextually accessible ways.

Let's take a moral issue and see how this matrix works—the epidemic of addiction. In 2019, we are currently in the largest overdose epidemic in US history. My younger brother died of overdose in September 2018 at thirty-four years old. Every day, more than one hundred thirty people in the United States die after overdosing on opioids.[25] How is the church responding to this horrible plight within our society? Obviously, my own experience shapes my passion here. In pioneer ministry, I often work in neighborhoods where prostitution, alcoholism, and addiction are prevalent. Scripture is always my starting point for understanding these addictions.

First, the value of "sober mindedness" and the dangers of addictive and related behaviors are mentioned throughout the entire scriptural witness (Prov 20:1, 23:20; Isa 5:11; 1 Pet 5:8; Gal 5:19-21; 1 Cor 6:18, 5:11, 3:16; Eph 5:18). The Bible warns us of the dangers of putting anything before God, which is a form of idolatry (Exod 20:3). It also speaks against gluttony (Prov 23:2). Second, church tradition informs us of the need for prudent stewardship over creation and care for the poor. Any activity that wastes exorbitant amounts of resources for the sake of pleasure is "a menace to society."[26] I referenced earlier the alcoholism epidemic of Wesley's

24. *The Book of Discipline, 2012* ¶104, p. 78.

25. Updated January 2019. https://www.drugabuse.gov/drugs-abuse/opioids/opioid-overdose-crisis#one

26. *The Book of Discipline, 2012,* ¶163.

day. He warned that the consumption of alcohol was dangerously inappropriate for Christians.[27]

Addiction preserves the cycle of extreme poverty for the masses and disproportional wealth for the few. Addiction destroys the possibility of being good stewards. Next, experience tells us engaging in addictive behaviors has paralyzing consequences, crippling any form of spiritual growth or compromising participation in a church community. Finally, reason is a strong tool in understanding and responding to addiction. The field of psychology has identified addiction as a disorder that has devastating consequences for the sufferers and their families. Addiction can lead to debilitating debt, familial neglect and abuse, divorce, violence, and incarceration.[28]

Hence, while some Christians can clearly drink responsibly, all Christians should work to help those caught in the addictive cycle. Our authentic response is one of words and deeds that promote the redeeming work of God into the sufferers' lives.[29] At each of the churches we've served, we've started Gamblers Anonymous/Gam-Anon, Alcoholics Anonymous/Al-Anon, and Celebrate Recovery programs. These accountability groups create safe havens for those afflicted. People we encounter in the recovery community are significantly more open to explore spiritual growth in a fresh expression than in the inherited congregations. Many accept Christ, find healing, and come into the life of the church through these contextual churches.

This is one way the people called Methodists can hold true to the living core of our faith and respond in a healing way with the redeeming love of God. The pioneers I work with find the quadrilateral to be a tremendous blessing in the practice of pioneer ministry. This compelling

---

27. John Wesley, 1748, *A Plain Account of the People Called Methodists.* John Wesley, 3 September 1732, Sermons, "On Public Diversions."

28. J. Butcher, S. Mineka, and J. Hooley, *Abnormal Psychology: Core Concepts* (Boston: 2008), 300.

29. *The Book of Discipline, 2012,* ¶163.

approach resonates with many in a post-Christian context, and positions Methodists to remix their vitality among emerging generations.

Field Story—Beck

When I was ten years old, Rev. Holland Vaughn looked into my eyes and said, "Michael, you are going to be a pastor one day." I found his pronouncement humorous, first, because I had no intention of ever becoming a pastor, and, second, because even at that age I was already running with neighborhood gangs and engaged in unholy activities. As the acolyte, week after week I carried my candle lighter and sat beside him at the altar. I watched the people laugh, cry, fall asleep, and occasionally shout an enthusiastic "Amen!" From the "preacher's bench" behind the pulpit, I observed this master using tradition, experience, and reason to bring the Bible to life. Subconsciously I was reasoning through my own theology, experiencing God's love through God's people, and absorbing the word from the biblical sermons, the creeds, and the hymns as we sung our faith together.

While my pre-adolescent experience of the church was that of a spiritual orphanage where I was loved, fed, and valued, this is not the experience of most people my age. "Dones" are people who many times carry the scars from church folks who harmed them (both real and perceived). It is common to hear the stories of how people weaponized the scriptures. The same Bible that gives us life can also inflict damage. This is why we need a community where we can "read, mark, and inwardly digest" the scriptures together, a place to wrestle with its truth and have conversations about its challenges and inconsistencies. Some of the most meaningful times in our fresh expressions are when we are engaging scripture. People are not afraid to ask questions, to go deeper, to see how the whole Bible is really about Jesus, and how it must be read through Jesus.

Denise is one of those people. She came from a tradition in which she was not encouraged to read the Bible for herself, and certainly not to question it. As she began to join us in our fresh expressions of church, she would throw truth grenades into the conversation. "Wait a minute. What? That doesn't make any sense." Or "That's stupid. How can that be true?" She was fond of saying things like that. I welcomed her comments because they forced us to look at our own assumptions. They made us re-think our "Christianese." I was there the first time Denise prayed out loud to a group, and it was beautifully honest, real, and powerful. Her relentless seeking is refreshing to us all.

After about a year of meeting in Burritos and Bibles, Denise decided she would plant her own fresh expression of church called Church 3.1. Denise has a passion for running; she does crazy long distances to prepare for marathons. Her fresh expression is a group of young professionals who gather to run a 5K race and then go back to work or home life. They gather, pray, run, and then come back and process what God has been up to in their lives since the last meeting. Part of that check in involves reading a couple of verses of scripture from their screens. I remember one gathering in which I looked over at Denise, a small woman, surrounded by mostly larger men deeply engaged in the fit culture network.

She was boldly leading us, sharing the truth that her engagement with scripture led her to. Not only had she wrestled with the Bible, but it had become so much a part of her that she was willing to lead others in the journey. Denise found a relationship with Jesus by searching God's word. She is now a bold pioneer who turned her passion into a form of church.

Missiography—Embodying the Message (Acevedo)

I've been on the same Bible reading program since 2002. So over seventeen years, I have read the Old Testament through once and the New Testament through twice. Late every August, the reading plan takes us through the book of Ezekiel and the book of Revelation. Both books are filled with confusing and wild imagery and frankly are hard even for the most seasoned follower of Jesus. I like to say, "Ezekiel and Revelation made lots of sense when I used to smoke weed."

So, the next time Ezekiel and Revelation came up in my reading, I honestly thought, "O Lord, not again." Seventeen years of this has gotten tough, but as the dutiful second son of a retired tech sergeant in the United States Air Force, I read it. And once again, the Holy Spirit broke through my objections and spoke a word. Below are the two texts the Holy Spirit "highlighted" for me and the observation, application, and prayer I wrote in my e-journal that morning, under the heading, "Embodying the Message."

"Fill your stomach with this," he said. And when I ate it, it tasted as sweet as honey in my mouth. (Ezekiel 3:3 NLT)

Then he added, "Son of man, let all my words sink deep into your own heart first. Listen to them carefully for yourself. Then go to your people in exile and say to them, 'This is what the Sovereign Lord says!' Do this whether they listen to you or not." (Ezekiel 3:10-11 NLT)

Ezekiel is called by God to be a spokesman for God. The people of Israel have strayed far from Yahweh and his ways. Ezekiel's calling is filled with a powerful metaphor. He must first eat then digest the message before he delivers it. The prophet must deeply ingest the Word of the Lord before he delivers it. And the message he gives will be a hard message to an even harder hearted people. Ironically, the New Testament reading was Revelation 2 where beginning here and for one more chapter, Jesus will deliver the good, bad, and ugly of seven churches to the seven churches. The preaching ministry is dangerous work that requires a deep embodying of the message for the preacher.

We are finishing the series on loving our neighbors at our church. It has been a hard word for God's people. We've shaken the people of God for four weeks about listening to the Holy Spirit and joining Jesus in loving all our neighbors, the stranger and those we would call "enemy." This series has not been about better communication or better sex. Getting this message about the stranger "in me" has been my personal challenge. In the words of John Wesley, "I love a commodious room, a soft cushion and a handsome pulpit." I like the safety of my sequestered office that is protected by four doors and lots of security. I love my gated community with my ADT protected alarm. Yet, the Holy Spirit keeps pushing me out of my safe places to "the zone of the unknown" to join Jesus in his mission of loving my neighbors, all my neighbors, my stranger neighbors and my strange neighbors and yes, even those I would call my "enemy." I hate when God wants me to "practice what I preach." I'd rather linger in my study over scripture, stand and deliver the message and go home for BBQ with my grandkids. But instead I signed up to be a reading mentor at the school and read with and to a third grader. This is just a start. Ugh!

Lord, help me deeply ingest your message before I give it to your people. At least let me be honest enough to admit when I am falling short of the requirements. Amen.

Missional Field Kit: Engaging Scripture with "Nones and Dones"

How do we study the Bible with people who have little to no experience with it?

Fresh Expressions UK and Fresh Expressions US have designed incredibly helpful apps called Godsend and FX Connect to help practitioners cultivate fresh expressions.[30] These would be great tools for your team.

One of the features of the apps is Michael Moynagh's set of simple questions to introduce someone to Jesus through Bible study. You could choose one Jesus story, read it together, and each week simply ask one of the following questions:

1. If this story happened today, what would it look like?

2. What does this story say to you?

3. How could this story make a difference in my life?

4. How did it make a difference?

(In the apps, you can find these questions in the "Share Jesus" section.)

---

30.   The Fresh Expressions UK Godsend App can be found at https://www.fxresourcing .org/godsend/share/. Also, the same material is available on the Fresh Expressions US App called "FX Connect."

Grace-Filled Waters and Open Table

Wesley considered the sacraments to be filled with mystery and the "ordinary channels through which God might convey to us...grace."[1] United Methodists across the theological spectrum agree that "There are two sacraments ordained of Christ our Lord in the Gospel; that is to say Baptism and the Supper of the Lord."[2] Wesley was convinced that the scriptural ordination of the two sacraments originated with Christ himself. Jesus commands his disciples to "go therefore and make disciples" by "baptizing them in the name of the Father and of the Son and of the Holy Spirit" (Matt 28:19 NRSV). Jesus instructs the disciples to partake of this meal (Matt 26:17; Mark 14:12; Luke 22:17) "in remembrance of me" (Luke 22:19; 1 Cor 11:24). Since the very first apostles, entrance through baptism was immediately followed with devotion "to the apostles' teaching, to the community, to their shared meals, and to their prayers" (Acts 2:41-42). Table fellowship has always been the center of Christian community and continues to be in fresh expressions of church.

The sacraments, as "outward signs of inward grace," are tangible objects highlighting spiritual realities. The grace-filled waters of our baptism

---

1. John Wesley, *The Standard Sermons in Modern English*, ed. K. C. Kinghorn, (Nashville: 2002), Vol. 1, 264.

2. *The Book of Discipline, 2012*, ¶103: XVI.

wash us clean, herald our new birth as children of God, and empower us to transform the world. True life begins in the waters of our baptism.[3] The grace-saturated meal presents our continual need for God and nourishes us for the journey. Bread and grape juice symbolize the graceful God who took on flesh and blood and "moved into the neighborhood" (John 1:14 MSG). I often explain the sacraments as ordinary presents, with extraordinary presence. These ordinary elements, infused with the Holy Spirit, point to the extraordinary nature of God's grace and mysterious activity in our lives. God engages our senses in each sacrament. In baptism, we see and hear the water trickling, and we feel it wash over us. In Holy Communion, we touch and taste the bread and juice as we search our hearts and confess our brokenness.

Besides the grace-filled dimension of baptism that precedes our own awareness, one of our distinct Wesleyan emphases is the *open table*.

For Wesley, Holy Communion was in one sense a sacrament of maintenance in which we *remember* our unification with Christ. Yet, more than a remembrance and short of transubstantiation, the Spirit makes the presence of Christ real in the elements. We partake, we drink, and we eat of his own living presence which sanctifies and sustains us (John 6:56-58). In a mysterious way, our spirits are nourished as grace is conveyed to us. We begin with confession and pardon, as we acknowledge "we have rebelled against your love."[4] And because Wesley believed this can be a moment of conversion, Holy Communion is a missional phenomenon.[5] Early Christians gathered around this meal in public spaces (1 Cor 11:17-34). Paul reminds us when we partake, it is a καταγγέλλω or *proclamation*: "you proclaim the Lord's death until he comes" (1 Cor 11:26 NRSV).

It is a frequent occurrence in fresh expressions that people receive Christ through partaking in the Lord's Supper for the first time. We've

---

3. Theodore Runyon, *The New Creation: John Wesley's Theology Today* (Nashville: Abingdon Press, 1998), 140.

4. *United Methodist Hymnal*, p. 12.

5. Runyon, *The New Creation*, 134.

heard something to the effect of, "When I tore the bread, I realized Christ died for me," many times. The graceful meal can both spark faith and sustain it. Further, our United Methodist tradition of an open table means that all are welcome no matter what their status may be.[6] Our inclusivity is based on the radical table fellowship of Jesus himself (Matt 9:10; Luke 15:2). No one is "worthy" to receive.[7] "We confess that we have not loved you with our whole heart.... We have not heard the cry of the needy."[8] It is a feast of forgiveness and acceptance, a foretaste of God's kingdom open to all sinners where we proclaim three essential truths: "Christ has died; Christ is risen; Christ will come again."[9] It is one of the channels through which this relentless, seeking God initiates a relationship with us.

These Wesleyan distinctives provide incredible missional potential for Methodist Fresh Expressions of Church, as well as some unique challenges. In Wesley's own day, there was serious controversy around lay preachers attempting to administer sacraments, something they had no authority to do under Anglican ecclesial authority.[10]

Time for a Remix

In Methodist circles, handling of the sacraments continues to be an area of contention. Often in our national trainings, people get to the *consecration dilemma*: "So if most people leading fresh expressions are laity, who is serving communion and conducting the baptisms?" The response to this question must be contextually sensitive.

---

6. Charles Wesley proclaims in "Come, Sinners, to the Gospel Feast": "let every soul be Jesus' guest. Ye need not one be left behind, for God hath bid all humankind" (no. 339 in *United Methodist Hymnal*, st. 1).

7. Charles Wesley, "Come Sinners, to the Gospel Feast": "the invitation is to all. Come, all the world! Come, sinner thou!" st. 2.

8. *United Methodist Hymnal*, 12.

9. *United Methodist Hymnal*, 14.

10. Ryan N. Danker, *Wesley and the Anglicans: Political Division in Early Evangelicalism* (Downers Grove, IL: IVP Academic, an imprint of InterVarsity Press, 2016), 19.

Let's start with the Lord's Supper. In The United Methodist Church, different bishops and conferences have different ideas about this, so I want to be careful not to make universal prescriptions. For instance, some are fine with an ordained elder "pre-consecrating" the elements before they are taken to the location. Others want the ordained person to be present during the gathering. Some churches are quite creative, taking the left-over elements from the traditional worship experiences and allowing the pioneers to serve them in the fresh expressions. If possible, having an ordained person is ideal; however, for churches that have multiple fresh expressions this may be unrealistic.

Regarding baptism, it doesn't seem like much of a challenge to get an ordained individual to preside. In many churches, baptisms are rare occasions.

For instance, in my role as cultivator of fresh expressions for the Florida Conference, I have observed this reality firsthand. In 2017, the FLUMC was comprised of six hundred twenty-five+ churches (+ correlates with multi-site scenarios). Of these, four hundred seventy-two churches were flat or declining in Average Worship Attendance (AWA) over the previous five years. Two hundred forty-two churches lost twenty percent of their membership, and two hundred seventy-two reported one or no baptisms. Three hundred four of the churches who lost AWA are in areas where the population is growing. In 2018, these trends continued with five hundred ninety-three church entities reporting End of Year Statistics. Of those, 64 percent were flat or declined in membership, and 69 percent were flat or declined in average worship attendance.[11]

In a smaller sample, the eighty-six churches in the North Central District (NCD) of Florida mirror the larger decline. Sixty-four of the eighty-six churches are plateaued or declining. Thirty-five of these churches are worshiping below fifty. Thirty-one congregations are in high risk scenarios, showing three or more risk indicators like declining worship, decreasing

11. Email correspondence with Steve Loher, Florida UMC Manager of Knowledge and Information Services on April 9, 2019.

finances, and no new members. Nineteen congregations had no baptisms or "professions of faith" in the last three years.[12] It could be argued that the handful of those that are growing in the attractional only mode are taking advantage of demographic trends, like retirement migrations or urbanization—already Christians moving into an area looking for a church.

Reaching and making new Christians is a pervasive challenge. These troubling statistics are not unique. Of the approximately thirty-three thousand United Methodist congregations in the United States, only five, or .01 percent, have been able to maintain an annual growth rate of 10 percent for the past ten years.[13] When people aren't being baptized into the faith, churches will decline.

Yet, there are also some positive developments from the North Central District as well. While at this point extraneous variables make it impossible to directly correlate fresh expressions activity with the revitalization of inherited congregations, twenty-two congregations are growing in worship attendance. Nine of those congregations (41 percent) have been experimenting with fresh expressions for the past four years. Each of those experimenting congregations grew in "professions of faith" and baptisms. They are among a handful of churches who are reversing decline by growing primarily through reaching out to the "nones" and forming new Christians.[14] Now beside eighty-six inherited congregations, over eighty fresh expressions have emerged.

The struggle over sacraments may be a little bit of history rhyming. Some have argued that the issue of sacraments actually led to the creation of a new denomination rather than a renewal movement within the larger church. As mentioned, not only did lay preachers serve the sacraments, as

---

12. Executive Summary. Collected by the FLUMC for the NCD in the 2018 Imprint Report.

13. Len Wilson, "Top 25 Fastest Growing Large United Methodist Churches, 2017 Edition," *lenwilson.us*. January 10, 2017, http://lenwilson.us/top-25-fastest-growing-large-umc-2017/.

14. Executive Summary. Collected for FLUMC NCD 2018 Imprint Report.

we will see in the next download, Wesley himself conducted ordinations outside the proper Anglican ecclesial channels.

Perhaps it is time for people in the Wesleyan tradition to rethink the idea of itinerant clergy serving circuits? Rather than understanding itineration in the institutional sense of being sent annually from one local church to another, local clergy now find themselves in communities where these strange circuits of fresh expressions are emerging. The ordained clergy could share the joy of visiting these emerging churches to provide the sacramental authority necessary. This is already starting to happen in the NCD.

I'm convinced that when we have an institutional log jam in sharing these grace-filled sacraments with all people, there are harder questions to ask. While I can't make general prescriptions for the whole church, I can share how we are navigating these challenges in the church I now lead, which is a traditional congregation and a network of fresh expressions.

Field Story—Beck

I mentioned earlier that once we had several fresh expressions up and running, we started to receive regular visitors back to our traditional worship service who would never return. This led to the creation of the New Life worship experience (a "fourth place," something in between what a person would experience in a fresh expression and a traditional worship experience). While our inherited church has grown, most of the growth is young families packing out New Life, which can feature social media moments, free breakfast, dance breaks, coffee toasts, arts and crafts, and interactive activities during the sermon to keep children and youth engaged.

Because most of those we reach in fresh expressions are new Christians, I have baptized many of the adults and nearly every child in that space. I have watched these families grow in the life of grace. Each week, it is typical to see children of every age, together with their families, receiving Holy Communion. With this surge of new believers, we are regularly explaining the meaning and significance of the sacraments, particularly the baptism of infants and the invitation of children *to* and the frequency *of* Holy Communion. "Nones" often question these practices, as do the "dones" (particularly those migrating from other theological persuasions). We welcome those teaching moments, which provide an opportunity to share our Wesleyan grace-centered understanding of the sacraments.

These "signs of grace" convey God's love into our lives in tangible ways. I frequently emphasize the "ordaining" aspect of baptism into the "priesthood of all believers."[15] Thus, through God's love, we are being initiated into the church, being cleansed from sin, being birthed anew as a child of God, and being claimed and empowered for Christian ministry in the world.[16] "Through baptism, you are incorporated by the Holy Spirit into God's new creation, and made to share in Christ's royal priesthood. We are all one in Christ Jesus."[17] They now belong to a new family, and have been given a new identity and a new mission.

However, most of our baptisms do not occur back at the main church facility. For instance, in 2019 over seventy persons were baptized, but only a handful on Sunday mornings. For example, one of our fresh expressions takes place in the local jail. A pastor friend recently went there to "share the gospel with the inmates." We refer to them as "men and women currently experiencing incarceration." He called me afterward to share that a number of them during the altar call proudly declared that they were "already Christians and members of Wildwood UMC." They had their membership certificates to prove this! Our approach has been long term relational witness, or an *incarnational* rather than *extractional* approach. So, we baptize as many people in the jail house as we do in the sanctuary back at the church compound. Because we really are a network of churches spread throughout our community, "WildOnes" are meeting in

---

15. Alan Hirsch and Dave Ferguson, *On the Verge: A Journey into the Apostolic Future of the Church* (Grand Rapids, MI: Zondervan, 2011), 266.

16. *The Book of Discipline, 2012*, ¶104, p. 72.

17. *United Methodist Hymnal*, p. 37.

places all throughout the community. We plant the seeds of the gospel, then let it grow wild.

At Wildwood, this is a key reason why we offer Holy Communion at every worship experience, including fresh-expression meetings in shelters, burrito joints, jail houses, rec centers, and tattoo parlors. Our time is always growing toward the table.

These celebrations also vary according to the context. At Tattoo Parlor Church, we gather in the waiting room of the parlor around a coffee table. We use a chalice and bread, but we don't recite the liturgy from a hymnal. We contextualize or "recode" the essential truth, moving through examination, confession, and pardon in the native language of tattoo culture. We emphasize the fact that we all feel shame, our not-enoughness. We also all make mistakes, we are pained by the hurt we cause (guilt), we commit to do better, and yet God loves us despite us and invites us to the table of grace. At Burritos and Bibles, we take an unleavened tortilla (probably closer to what Jesus used!), break it, and dip in the Hi-C from the Coke machine. We offer the elements to everyone gathered in the restaurant. Again, we recode the essential truth of the meal in a contextually faithful way. Many people have come to faith through communion, including staff, visitors, and patrons who randomly happened into the space.

Since Jill and I can't be at every fresh expression every time they gather, we do consecrate the elements in advance for our pioneers to distribute. The pioneers let those gathered know that the bread and juice were prayed over in advance by their pastors.

For us, anything that does not include or is not growing toward sacraments can scarcely be called church. We cherish our original Wesleyan appreciation of the sacramental life and returning to it through fresh expressions has become an igniting spark in the roaring blaze of revival to come. As Methodists, we practice varying forms of baptism and communion, and the amount of water or type of bread is not as important as the meaning, and what the Spirit is up to in our brokenness amid the mystery. Through fresh expressions we are catching a glimpse of the early church as a vibrant movement of entire families (households) being baptized, gathered around the Lord's Table, in all kinds of places, with all kinds of people (Acts 2; 16; 18).

Missiography—Missional Hospitality (Acevedo)

The waters of baptism, and the open table, are places of God's missional hospitality. The sacraments are means through which our other can be invited into the community.

The writer of Hebrews wrote to first-century Jewish followers of Jesus who witnessed the cruel harassment of fellow Christians by the Romans. To protect their hearts from growing stale and cynical, the writer invites Jesus's followers to go the extra mile and offer hospitality to the stranger. In Hebrews 13:2, the writer says, "Do not neglect to show hospitality to strangers, for by doing that some have entertained angels without knowing it" (Heb 13:2 NRSV). The Greek word for showing hospitality is *philoxenias*, which can mean showing love and hospitality to anyone. What's distinct about its use here is the compound meaning "love of strangers." Jewish followers of Jesus probably recalled the story in Genesis 18 when Abraham was hospitable to three strangers who showed up at his tent. In the story, Abraham did six things:

- ran to greet them (18:2)
- bowed down before them (18:2)
- provided water to wash their feet (18:4)
- gave them a place to rest (18:4)
- fed them a feast of high quality bread, meat, and dairy (18:5-8)
- escorted them down the road as they left (18:16)

These were exemplary acts of hospitality, and here's the twist in this story: "The Lord appeared to Abraham at the oaks of Mamre while he sat at the entrance of his tent in the day's heat. He looked up and suddenly saw three men standing near him" (Gen 18:1-2).

Who appeared before Abraham? The Lord! The storyteller goes on to describe three men showing up at his tent. He links together God's appearance to Abraham and Abraham's hospitality to the three strangers. Abraham was hospitable to God while being hospitable to the three strangers! Could it be that some of us do not experience the presence of God in our lives because we do not practice hospitality to the stranger? When we practice Christian hospitality to the stranger, we do it to God. Jesus picks up on this theme in Matthew: "I assure you that when you have done it for one of the least of these brothers and sisters of mine, you have done it for me" (Matt 25:40).

Hospitality with the stranger in the Bible pushes us beyond comfortable North American suburban niceties. It invites us into "the zone of the unknown" where our amazing and supernatural God loves to show up and show off. And in the process of showing hospitality, we address the greatest disease of our generation—loneliness. The sacraments cannot be enshrined and hidden from strangers in our neighborhoods and networks. We need to find ways to make them accessible to all.

This is why God continues to push me out of my comfortable office and gated community. Also, God continues to release our people to go be church with those outside the church. It's missional hospitality.

Missional Field Kit
Some Remixing

1. With your team, write out a list of common items in the church that have symbolic meaning. Perhaps do a field trip in the sanctuary. A list may include: cross, organ, hymnal, candles, pew, altar, robes, offering envelope, guitar, drums, *Book of Common Worship*, *Book of Discipline*, laptop, speaker, chalice, umbrellas, and so on.

2. Pair up in teams and try to create as many alternative uses for these items as possible. Take two minutes for each item (for

instance, hymnal: doorstop, weapon, height increaser, scrap paper, kindling, yard ornament, closet filler, and so on).

3. Discern together as a team: What other symbolic meaning might those items have for people outside the church?

4. Using only items familiar to those outside the church, what items might have symbolic meaning for them? (For instance, football, racecar, iPhone, coffee cup, instruction manual, lawn mower, movie theater seat, barstool, and so on.) How might you build bridges of meaning between those symbols? Or how might you translate the meaning of the items of the church world to the items of their world?

A Mission with a Church, Not a Church with a Mission

God has a mission; thus, there is a church. John Wesley understood the church in an instrumental way, as "the redeemed and redeeming fellowship." The church does not have a mission; it is God's missional instrument.[1] "Mission does not come from the church; it is from mission and in light of mission that the church has to be understood."[2] The church flows from the mission of God, "misson...is prior to the church, and is constitutive of its very existence."[3] Mission should birth structures "as mission takes shape so does the church." Structures should enable mission.

Early Methodism was the "missional church" movement of its day. Thus, the structure and polity of Methodism was birthed in the process of mission. Ultimately missionary need gave rise to different forms of order. Wesley's "practical divinity," his focus to share the gospel in "plain words

1. Stephen B. Bevans and Roger Schroeder, *Prophetic Dialogue: Reflections on Christian Mission Today* (Maryknoll, NY: Orbis, 2011), 15.

2. Jürgen Moltmann, *The Church in the Power of the Spirit: A Contribution to Messianic Ecclesiology* (Minneapolis: Fortress, 1993), 10.

3. Stephen B. Bevans and Roger P. Schroeder, *Constants in Context* (Maryknoll, NY: Orbis, 2004), 13.

for plain people" in the "fields" (spaces and rhythms) of their everyday lives, emerged as a nascent expression of the church.

Wesley re-appropriated the first principles of scripture around leadership structure for the movement. He was convinced that there was no clear biblical blueprint regarding church order, and that missionary need precipitates new forms. While his description of the threefold ministry (bishop, deacon, elder) was indeed scriptural, he also held that "bishops and presbyters are (essentially) of one order."[4] Thus, in his thinking, an elder could ordain if warranted by missional necessity.

Wesley here rested on the tradition of the early church fathers. In the scriptural allusions we see the terms *bishop* and *elder* used to describe local church leaders interchangeably. Ignatius of Antioch, writing just before his martyrdom in 110 CE, shows us how the threefold leadership arrangement functioned in the early church. In his letters, we discover that each local church had the same structure, with a bishop, assisted by a group of presbyters or elders, together with a group of deacons.[5] These positions were localized within each congregation. Thus, the Scriptures and some of the earliest voices from church tradition reveal something different than the medieval Christendom leadership structure still operating today.

While Wesley himself was an ordained priest in the Church of England, within the Methodist movement he actually functioned as a kind of "bishop" (*episcope*). While this role had taken on new institutional dimensions in Wesley's day, in the scriptural sense it was a function of "watching over" the flocks. Many of the leaders of the Methodist societies functioned in the biblical sense as "deacons" (*diakonia*), the "servant ministers" of the movement. The traveling preachers served in the role of "elders" (*presbyteros*) or in a "priestly function," though most had no formal institutional or educational credentials to serve in this way. They would probably be more analogous to "local pastors" than the "elders" in Methodism today.

4. John Wesley, *The Works of John Wesley* (Nashville: Abingdon Press, 1984). Journal, 20 January 1746; Wesley 1975: xx: 112.

5. Marcellino D'ambrosio, *When the Church Was Young: Voices of the Early Fathers* (Cincinnati, OH: Servant Books, 2014), 26.

The reality of a Methodist "bishop" was also born from a missional imperative. As Methodism spread over to the United States and began to take on a life of its own, out of sheer missional necessity to have a leader who could administer the sacraments, Wesley consecrated Thomas Coke as a "General Superintendent," and then instructed Coke to consecrate Francis Asbury in 1784. Many interpret this action as the defining act that, regrettably for Wesley, created a distinct denomination.[6]

Charles Wesley, who was experiencing an increased strain on his relationship with his brother John because of these progressively innovative acts, was becoming more and more disillusioned with the emerging movement. Following these consecrations, Charles apparently was not too thrilled with this activity, so he chided his brother openly and publicly in a published poem which read:

> So easily are bishops made
> By man's or woman's whim?
> W[esley] his hands on C[oke] hath laid,
> But who laid hands on him?[7]

These consecrations occurred outside the realm of appropriate authority in the Anglican Church. John Wesley used the scriptural rationale in cases of necessity to validate his actions, as he went back to first principles beneath the traditions. One missional need pertained to providing the sacraments to the new missional frontier.[8]

Asbury was never comfortable with the title of bishop, and the office today is very different than the role he played. Asbury was a pioneer missionary, who oversaw the work of planting and organizing Methodist circuits to meet the emerging need of the mission field. In some jurisdictions, candidates run political campaigns to get elected to an office and serve as a corporate CEO. However, let's restore the role through the

---

6. Richard P. Heitzenrater, *Wesley and the People Called Methodists* (Nashville: Abingdon Press, 1995), 286–88.

7. Heitzenrater, *Wesley and the People Called Methodists*, 286–88.

8. Heitzenrater, *Wesley and the People Called Methodists*, 286–88.

missional imperative of Wesley's day. A resident bishop is appointed to a specific episcopal "area" as a missional strategist. Missional leaders serve to catalyze movements and organize local leadership to advance the mission.[9]

John Wesley advised American Methodists to follow the scriptures and the primitive church.[10] He was both an Anglican priest and the founder of Methodism until the day he died. He provoked an awakening while tethered to the inherited church in Great Britain. He also blended the rules. To truly become a "mission with a church" some rule blending seems necessary within Methodism for inherited and emerging modes of church to live together.

Time for a Remix

Archbishop Rowan Williams used his role to foster the seeding of the Fresh Expressions movement in the United Kingdom. He coined the phrase a "mixed economy of church." Williams also frequently exclaims, "It's not the Church of God that has a mission, but the God of mission who has a church." The Fresh Expressions movement is awakening an instrumental understanding of the church again. It is not God's job to serve the church; the church is an instrument in the hand of a missionary God.

In the Fresh Expressions movement, we return to a minimalist definition of the church, based primarily in the "first principles" of scripture. These essential "marks" were formalized in the Nicene Creed in 381 CE as *one, holy, apostolic, catholic.* In fresh expressions language, we appropriate and remix those words to speak of the essentials as *inward, upward, outward,* and *ofward.*[11]

---

9. Alan Hirsch, Tim Catchim, and Mike Breen, *The Permanent Revolution: Apostolic Imagination and Practice for the 21st Century Church* (San Francisco: Jossey-Bass, 2012), 214.

10. Paul D. Avis, *The Oxford Handbook of Ecclesiology* (Oxford: Oxford University Press, 2018), 332.

11. Travis Collins, *From the Steeple to the Street: Innovating Mission and Ministry through Fresh Expressions of Church* (Franklin, TN: Seedbed Publishing, 2016), 179.

Inward: a community of believers unified *in* the faith, living *in* the one Lordship of Jesus Christ.

Upward: we grow *up* in worship of the one true God, seeking to reflect God's own character through our love for God and neighbor.

Outward: a community sent *out* in mission to the world together.

Ofward: we belong to a universal connection *of* Christians throughout all space, time, race, and nation.

Denominations have taken the three scriptural leadership roles of elder, bishop, and deacon, and arranged them in a pyramidal corporate hierarchy. Steven Croft advocates for a rediscovery of the value of these three leadership roles in a local context. He associates the three groups in the following way:

1. deacon (*diakonia*), the servant ministry of the church with pioneers;

2. elder (*presbyteros*), or priestly function of the church enabling and sustaining both inherited and emerging forms of church;

3. bishop (*episcope*), the watching-over function of the church, those who exercise collaborative oversight of areas with multiple parishes.

He also argues that we continue to need lay, licensed, and ordained individuals, for the full health of the mixed economy.[12] Local clergy persons overseeing inherited congregations and networks of fresh expressions need to understand themselves again as quasi-bishops, whose role is to equip the whole people of God to be missionaries in the fields.

Traditions with respect to roles and structures are simply innovations that hardened. I often remind folks in my denomination that we

---

12. Steven J. Croft, *The Future of the Parish System: Shaping the Church of England for the Twenty-First Century* (London, UK: Church House, 2006), 78–90.

Methodists are hard-wired for mission, but the movemental impulses are only somewhat preserved in the various institutional structures.

Methodists are indeed part of the larger *one, holy, apostolic, catholic* church at large,[13] and we also have a distinct missional identity among that larger body (1 Cor 12:12-26). We are a particular set of "body parts" among the body, while sharing in the fullness of that greater nature (1 Cor 12:12-26). Since Methodism was born from a missional imperative rather than doctrinal disputes, "our roots as a missional renewal movement are at the heart of our ecclesiology."[14]

Bishop Kenneth H. Carter, speaking to the leaders during an annual conference in 2014 said, "The time of the professional minister is over— the time of the missionary pastor has come." That pronouncement set me free, and I have been living into it ever since. At each of the churches I have served, I found a handful of people clinging to life and remembering the "good old days." Essentially, we have planted new churches in the midst of the old ones with the help of a minority of faithful folks. A new creation emerged through the synergistic relationship between those churches. The last thing they needed was a "professional minister" to hold their hand as they died. Instead, they needed a "missionary pastor" to lead them out to be the church. Furthermore, this is not the "pastor's job." The loss of the fivefold ministry from Ephesians 4:1-16 is in a large part responsible for the massive decline of pastor-centered Christianity in the West.[15]

The term *missionary-pastor* belongs together as a compound word, as demonstrated in the person of Christ who was both "the good shepherd" (John 10:11) and a missionary (Luke 15:4) who came to "seek and save the lost" (Luke 19:10). Jesus is the fullness of the fivefold ministry. He is the totality of what an apostle, prophet, evangelist, shepherd, and teacher can and should be. In Ephesians 4, a letter that circulated to many

---

13. *The Book of Discipline, 2012,* ¶103, Article V, P. 67.

14. *The Method of Our Mission: United Methodist Polity & Organization* (Nashville: Abingdon Press, 2014), 5.

15. Hirsch, Catchim, and Breen, *The Permanent Revolution,* 5–9.

churches, it takes all of us—collectively—to make one Jesus. Together, the Holy Spirit empowers "God's people for the work of serving and building up the body of Christ until we all reach the unity of faith and knowledge of God's Son. God's goal is for us to become mature adults—to be fully grown, measured by the standard of the fullness of Christ" (Eph 4:12-13).

As Vincent Donovan discovered, the "priesthood" as we know it is an example of culturization originating from the "Graeco-Roman world," not the New Testament. All faithful expressions of the church should be a result of this culturization process (the gospel being planted and growing wild in a context). Yet this requires a contextually appropriate version of a priesthood to grow organically out of those soils: "Continuing the process with a Western version of the priesthood renders the goal of an adult, indigenous, independent church virtually impossible."[16]

This is what's happening now in fresh expressions, as indigenous leaders in the group rise to become the "priest" of the community. Indeed, this is what John Wesley himself did in the cultivation and organization of the lay preachers. Again, our missional heritage flows from a people who saw that "the world is our parish" and every one of us had a part to play.

At Wildwood, after visiting each member in their homes, I literally took my office door off the hinges, placed it in the sanctuary, and preached a series called "Open Door Policy." I lovingly reminded folks I was sent to serve the community as a missionary pastor, not simply the church as personal chaplain.

We now regularly hold what we call "body-building gatherings." As the body of Christ, we acknowledge each of us serves specific functions within that body (1 Cor 12:27). We focus on our call as the "priesthood of believers" (1 Pet 2:4-10). Each of our leaders takes a battery of assessments, including spiritual gifts, APEST (a profiling instrument designed to help identify your ministry style in relation to the philosophy of the fivefold ministry of Ephesians 4[17]), and Gallup's StrengthsFinder. We

---

16. Vincent J. Donovan, *Christianity Rediscovered* (Maryknoll, NY: Orbis, 2003), 112.

17. https://www.theforgottenways.org/what-is-apest.aspx.

enter those results into a spreadsheet, and we use team-building resources to understand and develop each other's unique roles. We are also shying away from the catch-all-title of "pastor" for all leaders because it has the baggage of the declining Christendom structures in the West.

The primary tasks of the church, developed around the mission of making disciples, are connected to its very being. Our theological task is to build disciples in a variety of environments and rapidly changing contexts.[18]

While programs and churches don't "make disciples" (the Holy Spirit does), earlier we reviewed how ministries like Celebrate Recovery (a faith application of the 12 Steps), can provide ministry contexts to facilitate the movement of people through the "waves of grace." We use Celebrate Recovery as a pathway for the messy relational process of disciple-making.

A typical week at Wildwood includes a lay-driven cooperative food pantry that feeds several hundred families, a clothing ministry, interracial unity gatherings, and numerous anonymous and lay-driven Christian recovery fellowships filling the classrooms. We partner with and house on our church property a residential faith-based rehabilitation center for men called House of Hope. Underground Seminary and other programs designed for people at different stages in the journey of grace meet both at the church and in public spaces. Three primary worship experiences gather on Sundays. Prayer gatherings and numerous cooperative outreach ministries, including a large jail ministry, take place as well. Personal and social holiness in the inherited church is still alive!

However, I see discipleship taking place more than anywhere else in our fresh expressions of church. It looks similar to those first Methodist gatherings in fields, barns, homes, theaters, and so on. For us, our fields are Moe's Southwest Grill, dog parks, recreation centers, hair salons, and tattoo parlors. People gather in those spaces, with a desire to "flee the wrath to come," or to recode that in common English, "to find healing from the isolation of a hyperconnected world." They honestly share

18. *The Book of Discipline, 2012,* ¶104, p. 75.

about their broken places, illicit affairs, struggles, and loss. A community of love surrounds them as they try to walk with Jesus and grow out of their destructive behavior patterns. Many become leaders in their own right, planting their own fresh expression of church, freely giving back the flame of God's love as they have received it.

Field Story—Beck

Wildwood is an old south Florida town, literally divided by railroad tracks. Like many similar old southern towns, racism and sexism are shadows that cling to the present. Wildwood UMC was planted in 1881 as a Methodist Episcopal South congregation, which was a denomination committed to the wrong side of the slavery issue. Honestly, one hundred fifty years later, churches on both sides of the tracks are complicit in preserving the racism and segregation in our community.

Because we are a mission with a church and not a church with a mission, our orientation is focused outward toward what God is doing in our community. It is not enough for us to simply have worship services on the fault lines of a segregated community. We don't believe this reflects the kingdom of God, and we wanted to break down those barriers and see healing come to our community.

Some African American leaders accepted an invitation to serve on our fresh expressions team, and we created habitats for imagination where we could dream together about ways we could heal the racial divide in our community. The genesis of an interracial coalition started with a Prayer Walk for Racial Peace. In a time of civil unrest, multiple allegations of police brutality, and tense race relations, approximately four hundred people gathered at Wildwood City Hall to pray and walk as a visible sign against injustice. People showed up by the bus load, ready to march. A pastor opened by reading scripture. Law enforcement and elected officials spoke beside clergy with one voice. Songs were sung, prayers were offered.

One of the clergy encouraged everyone gathered to find a person they didn't know with a different skin color, embrace them, give them a phone number and call them tomorrow. Outside city hall, the kingdom of God broke into the world in a fresh way, as people embraced, connected, and relationships began. Someone showed up with cupcakes and a love feast erupted! I think the cupcakes were the sacraments that day—the shared bread that we broke.

We walked in prayer from city hall down Martin Luther King Jr. Boulevard—hundreds of people marching together, singing, laughing, holding hands.

We stopped our procession on the corner of Jackson Street. There, at a community center, in the epicenter of violence and drug activity in Wildwood where a string of drug-related murders had recently occurred, we once again paused to pray, sing, and connect as the Holy Spirit flowed through and among us. More and more people began to join us from the neighborhood. I had a feeling that this is what Wesley experienced in the fields of his day.

To see law enforcement and community alike lay aside our differences and pray for and with each other was significant. I have never witnessed such a tangible moment of healing and reconciliation among a crowd: neighbors praying over the officers they once saw as the enemy, officers embracing people they had arrested a time or two. This was the new creation breaking into Wildwood.

Then God did something special for us. From the makeshift stage of a trailer bed, a huge double rainbow appeared over our gathering. An eruption of cheers, joyful applause, hugging, and weeping ensued. The day concluded with that rainbow, the brightest double rainbow most of us had ever seen, a sign of God's covenantal promise of a new beginning.

There was no violence. There was no protest. Nothing controversial, except the controversial love that we shared.

We agreed that Jesus didn't wait back at the synagogue—he went to where the people were experiencing crisis and met their need. We agreed prayer must be combined with decisive action. We reached out to more clergy friends and created the Wildwood Clergy Coalition, an interracial group of church leaders focused specifically on opening to systemic kingdom change in our community.[19]

Sin manifests its harm through our many *isms*: racism, sexism, alcoholism, nationalism, presentism, and so on. Yet God wants to heal and restore us from this fragmentation through relationship. Something supernatural happens when we come together with our perceived other. We are healed from our isolation together. When we take it to the fields, God's Spirit is poured out on us in fresh ways. The prayer walk created a network of relationships and racial unity in our community. So when events like Charlottesville occurred, we were prepared to act prayerfully and decisively. We held a week-long citywide revival, and we are intentionally gathering at each other's churches to fellowship, eat, worship, and strategize together. Wildwood is a different kind of community today, as we intentionally seek to deal with the sore of racism. God is turning our mess into a masterpiece. The most incredible result of this focus has been the network of multiethnic fresh expressions that were born.

Missiography—Bumping into Mr. Wesley[20] (Acevedo)

In the summer of 2013, I was on a four-month sabbatical. I had been honored and humbled to receive a sizable grant that allowed my wife Cheryl and me over eight weeks to trace the life of Jesus in Israel; Paul in Italy, Greece, and Turkey; and the Wesleys in England, Scotland, Ireland, and Northern Ireland. We saw firsthand that Methodism is not just a church with a mission, but a mission with a church.

On one particular day, Cheryl and I were in Northern Ireland, in the small hamlet of Downpatrick, the burial city of the great St. Patrick. Upon

19. http://freshexpressionsus.org/2017/09/06/fresh-approach-charlottesville/.

20. This also appears in my book *Neighboring*.

167

arriving, we made our way into the parking lot of The St. Patrick Centre. The museum curator told us that our experience at the museum would be more helpful if we first toured St. Patrick's Cathedral and visited the grave of St. Patrick in the churchyard. So we exited the center, turned right, and made an immediate right to walk up a concrete path and ascended a hill to the cathedral. As we began to make our short ascent to the cathedral, we bumped into a delightful group of tourists who were gathered around a marble inset in the sidewalk. It was covered with debris and they were sweeping it off with their feet to read the inscription. Cheryl and I stepped around them and continued to make our climb.

When we arrived at the top of the small hill, we noticed another marble insert in the path that like the one below was covered with leaves, sticks and dirt, so we too began to sweep it off with our feet. Much to our delight, we read these words from John Wesley's journal from June 10, 1785:

> We came to Downpatrick where the preaching house being too small, we repaired, as usual to the Grove; a most lovely place, very near the most venerable ruins of the cathedral.

We looked around and with delight, we were standing in the grove where John Wesley preached! For a United Methodist preacher to happen upon a site where John Wesley actually preached was like a child's first visit to Disney World. I was giddy. I said to Cheryl, "You go inside the cathedral. I'm going to roll around in the grass and pray that the anointing of John Wesley falls upon me." It was a serendipitous gift of God.

When our sabbatical finished, I had time to reflect on the Wesley plaque and the grove where he preached. For most of the Methodist movement during John Wesley's life, the headquarters were in London and Bristol. We used planes and trains to get from England to Downpatrick in Northern Ireland!

Yet John Wesley traveled with a band of missionaries on horseback and by foot. He did this without the advantage of social media or a GPS. He did not have a laptop, smart phone, or tablet. He wrote letters and pamphlets to communicate to the people called Methodists and he led a fresh expression of church movement with followers of Jesus who transformed Great Britain on horseback!

By the time of John Wesley's death, there were nearly 115,000 people in the Methodist discipleship movement in the United Kingdom and Americas![21] United Societies with class meetings and bands sprung up all over England, Scotland, and Wales and then jumped the Irish Sea to Ireland. Later, Thomas Coke and Francis Asbury would champion the Methodist movement in America.

Missional Field Kit

This is the process for how fresh expressions usually develop:

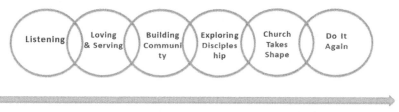

underpinned by prayer, on-going listening, and relationships with the wider church

Stage 1: Listening

The first stage of cultivating fresh expressions involves prayerful listening: to God, the inherited congregation, and the larger community.

Stage 2: Loving and Serving

This is simply about finding ways to be with people in our community, loving and serving them with no agenda.

---

21. www.christianitytoday.com/history/people/denominationalfounders/john-wesley .html.

Stage 3: Building Community

Through the repeated patterns of withness, the loving and serving grows into authentic community. A profound sense of connectedness begins to form, perhaps as we gather around the habitual practices. The relationships have grown beyond whatever hobby, passion, or activity may have initially connected the group.

Stage 4: Exploring Discipleship

Here the group begins to intentionally explore the Christian faith. This occurs through a mixture of both formal learning (intentional conversations) and social learning (simply sharing in the rhythms of life together).

Stage 5: Church Taking Shape

People are beginning to enter and sustain a relationship with Jesus Christ. The marks of the church begin to become a kind of compass for the journey: *one, holy, apostolic, catholic*—in fresh expressions language: *inward, upward, outward,* and *ofward*. (A community unified *in* the faith, growing *up* in worship and holiness, sent *out* in mission to the world, *of* a universal communion of believers throughout all space, time, race, and nation.)

Stage 6: Do It Again

Fresh expressions are born pregnant. Once a couple are growing, they begin to multiply. People start to realize, "If so and so can do that...I can do this." If Larry can turn his passion for taking his dog to the dog park into church, I can turn my passion for yoga into church. If church can happen while we run a 5K, it can happen at my workplace, and so on.

1. Where is your team in the process of the fresh expression journey?

2. How might we move to the next stage in the process?

3. Who will be responsible for taking next steps?

God of the Dumpster Dive

Even from the beginnings of the Holy Club at Oxford, there was a deep concern for those experiencing poverty:

> To devotional exercises was added charitable service amongst the underprivileged. Prisons and workhouses were visited. The sick and the poor were assisted. Wesley had a heart for the disadvantaged that would continue throughout his ministry. Wesley reported how "foul" the places he was preaching were from time to time. The kinds of people his ministry attracted included thieves, prostitutes, and those experiencing alcohol addiction. He did not just tolerate "those people," he loved them. Again, "I bear the rich and love the poor.[1]

For the early Methodists, God was present in the "dumpster dive." A seeking and sending God of relentless love visits dumpsters to recover what others have thrown away. God, like a good shepherd, leaves the ninety-nine to go after the one (Luke 15:4). This is a God who gets down on her hands and knees until she finds a lost coin (Luke 15:8). God is like a father who runs toward a prodigal son while he is still "a far way off" (Luke 15:20). The God of resurrection takes what's decaying, broken, dead, and makes it "new creation." Not one day, by and by, but right now.

---

1. Arthur S. Wood, *The Burning Heart: John Wesley, Evangelist* (Minneapolis: Bethany Fellowship, 1978), 38, 111, 137, 142.

Charles Wesley invites us to sing, "In Christ, your head, you then shall know, shall feel your sins forgiven; anticipate your heaven below, and own that love is heaven."[2] To be in a relationship with God, to love one's neighbor, this is the taste of heaven. It was a pervasive belief among those first Methodists that the new creation is unfolding now. Love awakened John Wesley's heart. Love sent him to the fields among the poor and marginalized. Perfect love of God and neighbor in this life by faith is a foretaste of God's kingdom come on the earth. The risen spirit of Jesus is available to be breathed in and received. God's kingdom is at hand and eternal life starts now. This is the blazing hope that shined in the darkness of the fields.

Wesley's message wasn't simply accepting Jesus now "to go to heaven when we die." The way to heaven was a journey that started in this life. It was this urgency and invitation that stirred folks to respond. It was this understanding that drove them into the societies to pursue this kingdom life now. The activity of early Methodists was shaped by this belief.

Time for a Remix

In a consumeristic culture of the network society, where everything is commoditized, individualized, and disposable, the dumpsters are full. A culture of consumerism creates a culture of waste. We throw away the outdated for the next new upgrade. We are caught up in a never-ending pursuit of the next newfangled thing. Unfortunately, not only do things become disposable in our system, but so do people. People who get in the way. People who don't contribute to our culture of sharing, remixing, and innovating.

In a culture obsessed with all new things, God makes all things new (Rev 21:5). God's way is not about discarding the old for the next new upgrade. God refuses to scrap the project in a dumpster and start over. God is a God of the remix, refreshing the existing material, reshaping

2.   "O For a Thousand Tongues to Sing" (no. 57), in *United Methodist Hymnal*, st. 7.

and recoding. God's way of "making all things new" is about resurrection. It's about empty tombs, marred clay reworked in the potter's hands, and healed lives. Resurrection is a power that breaks death, reverses the process of decay, recycles refuse, and makes churches come back to life. God is making the cosmos new in this way, right now (Rom 8:19-23).

I was involved in a substance-abuse intervention that resulted in a very public, miraculous healing. I was contacted by a family to lead a last-chance intervention for their son Jeff. The kingdom of God showed up in an apartment that smelled like feces and booze that morning, when he said, "Yes" to some help. After taking him to the facility the family had in place, he was immediately transferred to the hospital, where he was given two months to live and sent to hospice.

His parents requested our team to pray over him. Within days he had an incredible turn around, was released from hospice, and entered a recovery program. Dubbed a modern day "Lazarus" because of the very dramatic nature of Jeff's healing, his story created a buzz on several front-page features.[3] Jeff became a leader at our church, which has become a station of hope for those struggling with addiction, and furthermore a sign and foretaste of God's kingdom.

"With other Christians we recognize that the reign of God is both a present and future reality. The church is called to be that place where the first signs of the reign of God are identified and acknowledged in the world.... We also look to the end time in which God's work will be fulfilled."[4] Jesus's preaching on God's kingdom, inextricably linked to his identity, was not about a "postmortem destiny" or an escape hatch from some evil universe but about "God's sovereign rule" showing up on this earth, here and now, as it is in heaven.[5]

---

3. If you are interested in learning more about Jeff's incredible healing and subsequent ministry, see: http://www.villages-news.com/thankful-for-a-second-chance-man-embarks-on-daily-lazarus-walk/.

4. *The Book of Discipline, 2012*, ¶101, p. 44.

5. N. T. Wright, *Surprised by Hope: Rethinking Heaven, the Resurrection, and the Mission of the Church* (New York: HarperOne, 2008), 18.

While Jeff is an extreme example, he is a living illustration of a Wesleyan understanding of how God's reign is spreading through creation. For some people, Jeff's nickname and subsequent ministry, the "Lazarus Walk" (John 11), illustrates God's incredible power to resuscitate those who are dead. Jeff's healing is a powerful example of someone who has entered into the eternal life now and has become a citizen of God's inbreaking realm. Jeff ultimately died years later as a sober Christian; after he surrendered to Jesus in that hospice bed, his life was transformed. He authored several Christian children's books. He made an impact in the lives of his family and community. He died anticipating with bold faith the resurrection life to come.

Displacing our hope for eternal life to some distant celestial shore, disembodied from our current physical state, is the same misconception Martha has in the Lazarus story when she says, "Lord, I know one day. . . ." But Jesus confronts her misunderstanding with a powerful truth: "I am the resurrection and the life; those who believe in me will never die" (John 11:21-27). Jesus comes to give us an eternal life now and share in unending relationship with God.

I have witnessed many stories like Jeff's: people who once seemed broken beyond repair are made new. When the lives of the lost and broken, rich and miserable, and incarcerated or addicted enter the Kingdom, die to self, and live for Christ, they are transformed into new creatures. They begin living presently in the newness of eternal life, giving themselves as the ingredients of God's cosmic renewal that will soon be fully realized.

This expectation is a regular activity in fresh expressions of church. "Dones," people who feel like the church's throw aways, are finding a relationship with God again. "Nones," people with slight awareness that something is missing in their lives, are finding meaning, purpose, and taking their place in God's great recovery effort. People who only saw a mess when they looked in the mirror, isolated in their shame, are hearing the Spirit whisper "masterpiece," "beloved," and "very good." People who will never walk into our Sunday morning church services are finding new life in Christ in the fields of their everyday lives. They are becoming "new creation" and becoming the ingredients of the cosmic work of renewal that God is up to.

A waste-saturated culture throws away the obsolete for the next new upgrade. Even people become disposable commodities, especially black and brown immigrants at our borders, or those whose housing has been monetized in for-profit prison systems, or our religious and political others, elderly saints who have lived beyond their "usefulness" and are now euthanized or warehoused in care facilities. Yet amid this great crisis of our age—the devaluing of human lives in a consumerist culture of extraction, commoditization, and violence—God is making the dumpster dive, and fresh expressions of church are God's hands and feet.

This is my hope for the people called Methodists. Although it seems the world has disposed of denominations in the ecclesial dumpster, God is calling us to join along in the dumpster-diving activities. Fresh Expressions is one of the powerful ways God is recovering lives that have been thrown away. This is the way forward to true revitalization: dying and giving ourselves away in this effort. Dying is actually a movement in the process of resurrection; a seed that never goes into the ground never produces fruit (John 12:24). As Jim Harnish says regarding church revitalization, *You Only Have to Die.*[6] Cultivating fresh expressions allows us to give ourselves away to our communities. It's allowing us to plant seeds of the gospel that will grow wild as an indigenous expression of the church in a post-Christendom network society. We hope this field guide will help you to join in.

Field Story—Beck

Jill Beck is the pioneer who leads one of our most incredible fresh expressions, Connect. Connect is a church that meets primarily with

---

6. James A. Harnish, *You Only Have to Die: Leading Your Congregation to New Life* (Nashville: Abingdon Press, 2004), 11.

children in the Martin Luther King Jr. Building on the west side of Wild-wood. The west side is primarily an African American community. This is the place where we ended our interracial unity march beneath the God-given rainbow described previously. Churches in the community collabo-rated to renovate that space. Now Jill and her dedicated team, collaborat-ing with our friends from other area churches, have turned that third place into a church on Saturday mornings. Mostly children and teens show up for food, games, and Jesus stories. Some of the children received their first Bible and discovered they were named after great prophets at Connect.

Jill is a pastor to that community. She can freely walk the streets, in-cluding some where drugs are sold and shootings occur. She is respected and even loved. Many times, the parents join and connect with a church for the first time. Sometimes police officers hang out at Connect, play games with the kids, cook, and throw the football. An amazing transfor-mation has happened. Children who once saw cops as "the enemy" have now decided they want to be law enforcement when they grow up! This fresh expression gave birth to a pilot junior cadet program to help those kids pursue that dream.

One Saturday, as we gathered for Connect, a sweet little girl who comes regularly showed up with a couple of her siblings. She started pass-ing out stickers from the arts and crafts table to selected individuals, in-viting them to her birthday party. As we inquired where and when her birthday party would take place, we discovered that there was no birthday party for her. But she was turning Connect into one! Some of our team asked her what she would want for presents, if she could have anything, and what kind of cake she liked. Jill ran to the store and grabbed these items. Next, we paused the experience to gather around the table as family and sing, "Happy Birthday." She ripped through her presents, blew out her candles, laughed, cried, and gave lots of hugs.

The guidance of the Holy Spirit is unpredictable like that. We may have a church program in mind, while the Spirit just wants to give his princess a birthday party. This is not a unique story when it comes to fresh expressions of church.

Again, fresh expressions are born pregnant; they multiply. One day, while my wife was leading Connect, some dealers from across the street came over and handed Jill a wad of cash. (Drugs are being sold across the street night and day.) She called, concerned about what she should do. I thought to myself, "This would be an interesting debate for a seminary class somewhere." But I simply responded, "Take it honey; it belongs to the kingdom now."

This opened the door for us to have a conversation with the group across the street. We went over to thank them for the contribution and let them know we would use it to buy Bibles and food for the children. They thanked us for being there, and for what we were doing in the community.

One thing I've learned about drug dealers is their incredible, God-given, entrepreneurial impulse. Many times, they are skilled marketers with great adaptive leadership capacity. They are often systematically oppressed and unable to obtain education or other basic opportunities afforded privileged (white) people. A group of us pastor friends began to wonder if church might be able to form here. Trap Stars for Jesus was born, a church for drug-dealers desiring to go legit.

Our basic approach is that we would talk about this guy Jesus half the time, and during the other half we would offer a Business 101 course with mentorship and resources on how to get a business license, identify niche markets, obtain equipment, workers compensation, and insurance. Imagine the systemic impact on the community as one drug dealer becomes a legitimate business owner. This is how a chain reaction of fresh expressions can occur, as we ask, "Who is our other? How can we bring healing to what is sore in our community?"

This is how our God of the "dumpster dive" works. God treasures the ones the world throws away. This is what a mission with a church looks like: Methodism remixed for the new missional frontier.

Missiography—An Egyptian Fresh Expression (Acevedo)

On July 13, 2016, as God continued to challenge my attractional-only church ministry, I sat down and read Isaiah 19. Here's what the Holy Spirit whispered to me:

> In that day there will be an altar to the LORD in the heart of Egypt, and there will be a monument to the LORD at its border. It WILL be a sign and a witness that the LORD of Heaven's Armies is worshiped in the land of Egypt. When the people cry to the LORD for help against those who oppress them, he will send them a savior who will rescue them. The LORD will make himself known to the Egyptians. Yes, they will know the LORD and will give their sacrifices and offerings to him. They will make a vow to the LORD and will keep it. The LORD will strike Egypt, and then he will bring healing. For the Egyptians will turn to the LORD, and he will listen to their pleas and heal them. (Isa 19:19-22 NLT)

Isaiah is communicating God's judgment on Egypt. This is the land and the people that welcomed Joseph, but when a Pharaoh ascended who did not know Joseph, he enslaved the Hebrews. Egypt had already experienced the judgment of God when Moses emancipated the people of God and drove them into the wilderness. Later, Egypt would be the land where our Savior was taken by his parents when they feared for Jesus's life. Now Egypt is in the crosshairs of a holy God. But these four verses intrigue me. Embedded in God's judgment is a promise. A witness to God will be found within the boundaries of Egypt. How cool is that? God will be worshipped within the land of the pagans. God will make sure there is a witness in the land that will cause Egyptians to turn to the Lord. This is an Egyptian fresh expression!

God is still challenging my attractional-only ministry models. I was operating with a ministry model based on "build it and they will come." Create a safe, healthy, Christ-centered church with good preaching and worship, exciting children's and youth ministry, life changing small groups, and effective outreach and your church will grow. And it did. Now I believe this is not the only model. Joining Jesus in his mission means we not only pray, "Lord, send us the people nobody else wants or sees," but it also means we add to our prayer, "Lord, send us to the people nobody else wants or sees." Creating spaces and places outside of our church for our people to disciple people in their culture is a newer concept for me. Embracing fresh expressions really isn't a big leap for our people. It's the important next step for us to be a church with a healthy and holy mixed economy of inherited, "come to us" church and a fresh expressions "go to you" church.

This has allowed us to join into the mission of our dumpster-diving God. Continue to guide us, Lord, into Egypt where we can establish places for your name to be honored and for people who are far from you to make vows to you. Amen.

Missional Field Kit: Recoding Exercise

With your team, consider together whether the people in your community are hearing your message as "good news." If we want emerging generations to hear God's news as good news, we should start where God starts... "very good."

As Jorge Acevedo often says, we need to share the good news not only where it is "good" but where it is also "news." How would you share the gospel with someone who has never heard it before? In a culture that communicates in tweets, how might you share the gospel in a concise but impactful way?

Here's a fun field kit exercise for your team to do together.

What Is the Good News?

Write a definition of the gospel in:

- 144 characters (Have each person on the team try to share the gospel in a "tweet.")

179

- 1 sentence (Have each person try to share the gospel in one sentence.)

- 3 words (Now try to share the gospel in three words!)

Reflect on your responses together.

A Mature Fresh Expression

How can your team know the difference between a "potential" and "mature" fresh expression? Or what indicators can we use to distinguish between, say, an outreach and a new church? I have developed the "Four C's" as a kind of guide to help:

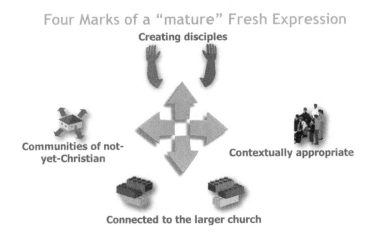

Four Marks of a "mature" Fresh Expression

Creating disciples

Communities of not-yet-Christian

Contextually appropriate

Connected to the larger church

Creating disciples: Disciples of Jesus Christ are being formed. This is not just playing church.

Communities of not-yet-Christians: These are gatherings with and for people who are not Christians yet. They are not just groups of already Christians hanging out in the community.

Contextually appropriate: This community has emerged organically from the context; it takes on the shape, patterns, and language of the people there. This is not planting our colonial "version of church" in foreign soils.

Connected to the larger church: The fresh expression is tethered to the inherited church in some relational way. These are not little colonies isolated from or in opposition to the inherited church.

With your team, talk through the Four C's. Do you see each one in the fresh expression(s) you are pioneering? If not, what could you do to grow in that area?

Credits

Arbuckle, Gerald A. *Refounding the Church: Dissent for Leadership*. Maryknoll, NY: Orbis, 1993.

Avis, Paul D. *The Oxford Handbook of Ecclesiology*. Oxford: Oxford University Press, 2018.

Backert, Chris. "Emerging Church and Missional Church: Same Difference?" *Fresh Expressions US*. April 18, 2016. http://freshexpressionsus.org/2016/04/18/emerging-church-missional-church-difference/.

Backert, Chris. https://freshexpressionsus.org/2018/12/10/fresh-expressions-us-year-end-review-2018/.

Baker, John. *Celebrate Recovery*. Grand Rapids, MI: Zondervan, 2012.

Baker, Jonny, and Cathy Ross. *The Pioneer Gift: Explorations in Mission*. Norwich, UK: Canterbury Press, 2014.

Beck, Michael. *Deep Roots, Wild Branches: Revitalizing the Church in the Blended Ecology*. Franklin, TN: Seedbed Publishing, 2019.

Beck, Michael. http://freshexpressionsus.org/2017/09/06/fresh-approach-charlottesville/.

Beck, Michael. https://freshexpressionsus.org/2018/03/05/history-repeating-discipleship/.

Bettenson, Henry S., and Chris Maunder. *Documents of the Christian Church*. Oxford and New York: Oxford University Press, 1999.

Bevans, Stephen B., and Roger P. Schroeder. *Constants in Context*. Maryknoll, NY: Orbis, 2004.

Bevans, Stephen B. and Roger Schroeder. *Prophetic Dialogue: Reflections on Christian Mission Today*. Maryknoll, NY: Orbis, 2011.

Bolger, Ryan K. "Practice Movements in Global Information Culture: Looking Back to McGavran and Finding a Way Forward." *Missiology* 35, no. 2 (2007): 181–93. https://journals.sagepub.com/doi/abs/10.1177/009182960703500 208?journalCode=misb.

Bolton, Bill, and John Thompson. *Entrepreneurs: Talent, Temperament and Opportunity*. London, UK, and New York: Routledge, 2013.

Bonhoeffer, Dietrich. *The Cost of Discipleship*. New York: Touchstone, 1995.

Bonhoeffer, Dietrich. *Life Together*. New York: Harper and Row, 1954.

Bosch, David J. *Transforming Mission: Paradigm Shifts in Theology of Mission*. Maryknoll, NY: Orbis, 1991.

Brafman, Ori, and Rod A. Beckstrom. *The Starfish and the Spider: The Unstoppable Power of Leaderless Organizations*. New York: Portfolio, 2014.

Brueggemann, Walter. *Finally Comes the Poet*. Minneapolis: Fortress, 1989.

Butcher, James N., Susan Mineka, and Jill Hooley. *Abnormal Psychology: Core Concepts*. Boston: Allyn and Bacon, 2008.

Carter, Ken. "Church Vitality." https://www.flumc.org/church-vitality.

Castells, Manuel. *The Rise of the Network Society*. Oxford and Malden, MA: Blackwell Publishers, 2000.

Chilcote, Paul W. *Active Faith: Resisting 4 Dangerous Ideologies with the Wesleyan Way*. Nashville: Abingdon Press, 2019.

Chilcote, Paul W. *John and Charles Wesley: Selections from Their Writings and Hymns*. Woodstock, VT: SkyLight Paths Publications, 2011.

Chilcote, Paul W. *Recapturing the Wesleys' Vision: An Introduction to the Faith of John and Charles Wesley*. Downers Grove, IL: InterVarsity Press, 2004.

Chilcote, Paul W. *The Wesleyan Tradition: A Paradigm for Renewal*. Nashville: Abingdon Press, 2002.

Clayton, M. Christensen, Michael E. Raynor, and Rory McDonald. "What Is Disruptive Innovation?" *Harvard Business Review*. December 2015. Accessed October 20, 2017. https://hbr.org/2015/12/what-is-disruptive-innovation.

Collins, Kenneth J. *The Theology of John Wesley: Holy Love and the Shape of Grace.* Nashville: Abingdon Press, 2007.

Collins, Travis. *From the Steeple to the Street: Innovating Mission and Ministry Through Fresh Expressions of Church.* Franklin, TN: Seedbed Publishing, 2016.

Cooper, Burton. *Why, God?* Atlanta: John Knox Press, 1988.

Cray, Graham. *Mission-Shaped Church: Church Planting and Fresh Expressions in a Changing Context.* New York: Seabury Books, 2010.

Cray, Graham, Ian Mobsby, and Aaron Kennedy. *Fresh Expressions of Church and the Kingdom of God.* Norwich, UK: Canterbury Press, 2012.

Croft, Steven J. *The Future of the Parish System: Shaping the Church of England for the Twenty-First Century.* London, UK: Church House, 2006.

D'Ambrosio, Marcellino. *When the Church Was Young: Voices of the Early Fathers.* Cincinnati, OH: Servant Books, 2014.

Danker, Ryan N. *Wesley and the Anglicans: Political Division in Early Evangelicalism.* Downers Grove, IL: IVP Academic, an imprint of InterVarsity Press, 2016.

Donovan, Vincent J. *Christianity Rediscovered.* Maryknoll, NY: Orbis, 2003.

Enns, Peter. *Inspiration and Incarnation: Evangelicals and the Problem of the Old Testament.* Grand Rapids, MI: Baker Academic, 2005.

Felton, Gayle C. *United Methodists and the Sacraments.* Nashville: Abingdon Press, 2007.

Frost, Michael, and Alan Hirsch. *ReJesus: A Wild Messiah for a Missional Church.* Peabody, MA, and Sydney: Hendrickson Publishers, Strand Pub, 2009.

Fujimura, Makoto. *Culture Care: Reconnecting with Beauty for Our Common Life.* New York: Fujimura Institute, 2014.

Goodhew, David, Andrew Roberts, and Michael Volland. *Fresh!: An Introduction to Fresh Expressions of Church and Pioneer Ministry.* London, UK: SCM Press, 2012.

Guthrie, Shirley C. *Christian Doctrine.* Louisville, KY: Westminster John Knox, 1994.

Hamilton, Adam. *Making Sense of the Bible: Rediscovering the Power of Scripture Today.* New York: HarperOne, 2014.

Harnish, James A. *You Only Have to Die: Leading Your Congregation to New Life.* Nashville: Abingdon Press, 2004.

Harper, S. *The Way to Heaven: The Gospel According to John Wesley.* Grand Rapids, MI: Zondervan, 2003.

Harper, Steve. *Devotional Life in the Wesleyan Tradition.* Nashville: Upper Room Books, 1995.

Haynes, Donald. *On the Threshold of Grace: Methodist Fundamentals.* Dallas: UMR Communications, 2010.

Heath, Elaine A., and Larry Duggins. *Missional, Monastic, Mainline: A Guide to Starting Missional Micro-Communities in Historically Mainline Traditions.* Eugene, OR: Cascade, 2014.

Heim, S. Mark. *Saved from Sacrifice: A Theology of the Cross.* Grand Rapids, MI: Eerdmans, 2006.

Heitzenrater, Richard P. *Wesley and the People Called Methodists.* Nashville: Abingdon Press, 1995.

Hirsch, Alan, and Dave Ferguson. *On the Verge: A Journey into the Apostolic Future of the Church.* Grand Rapids, MI: Zondervan, 2011.

Hirsch, Alan, Tim Catchim, and Mike Breen. *The Permanent Revolution: Apostolic Imagination and Practice for the 21st Century Church.* San Francisco: Jossey-Bass, 2012.

Hirsch, Alan. *5Q: Reactivating the Original Intelligence and Capacity of the Body of Christ.* USA: 100M, 2017.

Hirsch, Alan. *The Forgotten Ways: Reactivating the Missional Church.* Grand Rapids, MI: Brazos, 2006.

Hodgett, T., and P. Bradbury. "Pioneering Mission Is…a Spectrum," *ANVIL* 34, no. 1. Accessed January 5, 2019. https://churchmissionsociety.org/resources/pioneering-mission-spectrum-tina-hodgett-paul-bradbury-anvil-vol-34-issue-1/.

Inbody, Tyron. *The Faith of the Christian Church: An Introduction to Theology* (Grand Rapids, MI: Eerdmans, 2005), 155–57.

Jones, Angela. *Pioneer Ministry and Fresh Expressions of Church.* London, UK: SPCK, 2009.

Jones, Scott J. *United Methodist Doctrine: The Extreme Center*. Nashville: Abingdon Press, 2002.

Küng, Hans. *The Church*. Garden City, NY: Image Books, 1976.

Laytham, D. B. *God Does Not Entertain, Play "Matchmaker," Hurry, Demand Blood, Cure Every Illness*. Grand Rapids, MI: Brazos Press, 2009.

Long, Thomas G. *What Shall We Say?: Evil, Suffering, and the Crisis of Faith*. Grand Rapids, MI: Eerdmans, 2011.

Maddox, R. *Responsible Grace: John Wesley's Practical Theology*. Nashville: Kingswood, 1994.

Maddox, R., and Runyon, T. *Rethinking Wesley's Theology for Contemporary Methodism*. Nashville: Kingswood, 1998.

Male, David. "Do We Need Pioneers?" 2017. https://freshexpressions.org.uk/get-started/pioneer-ministry/.

Male, David. *Pioneers 4 Life: Explorations in Theology and Wisdom for Pioneering Leaders*. Abingdon: Bible Reading Fellowship, 2011.

McGavran, Donald A. *The Bridges of God: A Study in the Strategy of Missions*. Eugene, OR: Wipf & Stock, 2005.

McGrath, Alister E. *Christian Theology: An Introduction*. Chichester, West Sussex, United Kingdom and Malden, MA: Wiley-Blackwell, 2011.

Migliore, Daniel L. *Faith Seeking Understanding: An Introduction to Christian Theology*. Grand Rapids, MI: Eerdmans, 2014.

Moltmann, Jürgen. *The Church in the Power of the Spirit: A Contribution to Messianic Ecclesiology*. Minneapolis: Fortress, 1993.

Moltmann, Jürgen. *The Crucified God: The Cross of Christ as the Foundation and Criticism of Christian Theology*. Minneapolis: Fortress, 1993.

Moynagh, Michael. *Being Church, Doing Life: Creating Gospel Communities Where Life Happens*. Oxford, England, UK and Grand Rapids, MI: Monarch, 2014.

Moynagh, Michael. *Church in Life: Emergence, Ecclesiology and Entrepreneurship*. London, UK: SCM Press, 2017.

Moynagh, Michael, and Philip Harrold. *Church for Every Context: An Introduction to Theology and Practice*. London, UK: SCM Press, 2012.

187

Credits

Moynagh, Michael, and Richard Worsley. *Going Global: Key Questions for the Twenty-First Century*. London, UK: A and C Black, 2008.

Murray, Ian. *Wesley and the Men Who Followed*. Edinburgh: The Banner of Truth Trust, 2003.

Murray, Stuart. *Church After Christendom*. Milton Keynes: Paternoster Press, 2004.

Nelstrop, Louise, and Martyn Percy. *Evaluating Fresh Expressions: Explorations in Emerging Church: Responses to the Changing Face of Ecclesiology in the Church of England*. Norwich: Canterbury Press, 2008.

Newbigin, Lesslie. *Foolishness to the Greeks: The Gospel and Western Culture*. Grand Rapids, MI: Eerdmans, 1986.

Newbigin, Lesslie. *The Good Shepherd: Meditations on Christian Ministry in Today's World*. Grand Rapids, MI: Eerdmans, 1977.

Oldenburg, Ray. *The Great Good Place: Cafés, Coffee Shops, Bookstores, Bars, Hair Salons, and Other Hangouts at the Heart of a Community*. New York and Berkeley, CA: Marlowe, Distributed by Publishers Group West, 1999.

Peterson, Eugene. *Eat This Book: A Conversation in the Art of Spiritual Reading*. Grand Rapids, MI: Eerdmans, 2006.

Rendle, Gilbert R. *Quietly Courageous: Leading the Church in a Changing World*. Lanham, MD: Rowman and Littlefield, 2019.

Roxburgh, Alan J. *Structured for Mission: Renewing the Culture of the Church*. Downers Grove, IL: InterVarsity, 2015.

Runyon, Theodore. *The New Creation: John Wesley's Theology Today*. Nashville: Abingdon Press, 1998.

Russell, Brian. *Realigning with God: Reading Scripture for Church and World*. Eugene, OR: Cascade, 2015.

Sarasvathy, Saras D. "What Makes Entrepreneurs Entrepreneurial?" https://dx.doi.org/.

Smith, Heather. "Inside America's Largest Religious Revival You Know Nothing About," *The Federalist*. November 2017. http://thefederalist.com/2017/11/10/inside-americas-largest-religious-revival-know-nothing/, Accessed November 2017.

Sweet, Leonard I. *The Greatest Story Never Told: Revive Us Again*. Nashville: Abingdon Press, 2012.

Sweet, Leonard I. *Me and We: God's New Social Gospel.* Nashville: Abingdon Press, 2014.

Sykes, Stephen, John E. Booty, and Jonathan Knight. *The Study of Anglicanism.* London, UK: SPCK/Fortress, 1998.

Tamez, Elsa. *The Amnesty of Grace: Justification by Faith from a Latin American Perspective.* Nashville: Abingdon Press, 1993.

Taylor, Paul. *The Next America: Boomers, Millennials, and the Looming Generational Showdown.* New York: Public Affairs, 2015.

The United Methodist Hymnal. Nashville: The United Methodist Publishing House, 1989.

Vocations to Pioneer Ministry. https://www.cofepioneer.org/assessment/.

Weems, Lovett H. *Focus: The Real Challenges That Face The United Methodist Church.* Nashville: Abingdon Press, 2011.

Wesley, John. *The Works of John Wesley.* Peabody, MA: Hendrickson Publishers, 1984.

Wesley, John, and Albert C. Outler. *John Wesley.* New York: Oxford University Press, 1964.

Wesley, John, et al. *The Works of John Wesley.* Nashville: Abingdon Press, 1984.

Willimon, William H. *This We Believe: The Core of Wesleyan Faith and Practice.* Nashville: Abingdon Press, 2010.

Willimon, William H. *United Methodist Beliefs: A Brief Introduction.* Louisville, KY: Westminster John Knox, 2007.

Willimon, William H. *Who Will Be Saved?* Nashville: Abingdon Press, 2008.

Willimon, William H. *Why I Am a United Methodist.* Nashville: Abingdon Press, 1990.

Wood, Arthur S. *The Burning Heart: John Wesley, Evangelist.* Minneapolis: Bethany Fellowship, 1978.

Wright, Christopher J. H. *The Mission of God: Unlocking the Bible's Grand Narrative.* Downers Grove, IL: InterVarsity, 2006.

Wright, N. T. *Surprised by Hope: Rethinking Heaven, the Resurrection, and the Mission of the Church.* New York: HarperOne, 2008.

Alternate Ending

On a landscape of decline, can your church experience an alternate ending?

I am one of those people who is consistently the last one to leave the movie theater. I always wait for all the credits to roll. Sometimes the movie was so touching that I need a couple of minutes to process it and identify places where I saw the Gospel. Sometimes there is a little trailer to a sequel, a final hidden scene, or an alternate ending. You have made it all the way to the credits of this story. After all is said and done, this is the question I want you to leave with: Can my church experience an alternate ending?

I know the frustration of giving your life for a church, giving your prime years, giving all you have, yet it continues to decline. I know about the sleepless nights, the neglected families, the constant state of fatigue. If you know those feelings, this book was really written for you. I wrote it because I honestly believe fresh expressions is the greatest hope for reaching people, transforming communities, and potentially revitalizing a congregation.

I have seen it work, and I have seen it fail. But God has recently brought to my awareness that what we consider failure on this side of eternity looks different from God's perspective.

I want to leave you with a final image to illustrate what I mean. An incredible book on polycentric leadership is Brafman and Beckstrom's

The Starfish and the Spider: The Unstoppable Power of Leaderless Organizations.[1] They offer examples of both centralized and decentralized leadership, analyzing them closely with a hybrid organization that very much resembles the blended ecology way. One of the most powerful lessons in the book was this: starfish and spiders may appear structurally similar, but there is a major distinction. When you cut the head off of a spider, it dies. However, when you cut a starfish in half, it replicates, becoming two starfish.

Some inherited congregations will die, no matter what we do. Unfortunately, it is usually the people in those congregations that will inadvertently cause their death. If they are not willing to die to self and open themselves to the resurrection power of the God who is making all things new, they may close. However, the blended ecology way leaves a new kind of church in the communities where the inherited congregation once was—a network of churches in the flows, which may become the future church of that community.

I don't know what will happen to the denomination I have given my life to serve. Yet, at the end of the day, measuring not the numbers but the stories, I have seen God retrieve so many once fragmented souls, heal them, and send them to change the world. That is the real legacy that we leave behind—transformed lives. It was Wesley's legacy as well. Whether the brick and mortar realities endure or not, the people that we share life with in these fresh expressions will continue to be the church where the church is not. Those that have heard the call and responded will be the cultivators who plant the seeds of what the church will be.

Give your energy to creating starfish, not spiders. Plant the seeds of trees you may never see grow. Boldly "futurefit" communities for the coming urban garden of new creation, where we will gather at the tree of life together again. It is my deepest prayer for you that your churches and communities will experience an alternative ending.

See you at the tree, my friends!

---

1. Ori Brafman and Rod A. Beckstrom, *The Starfish and the Spider: The Unstoppable Power of Leaderless Organizations* (New York: Portfolio, 2014).